To TARA,
FOOD IS LOVE!

DOUBLE
HAPPINESS

TREVOR LUI Host of Soulful Food Stories

THE DOUBLE HAPPINESS

COOKBOOK

88 Feel-Good Recipes and Food Stories

Figure 1
Vancouver / Berkeley

Cataloguing data are available from Library and Archives Canada
ISBN 978-1-77327-136-1 (hbk.)

Design by Naomi MacDougall
Hand lettering by Ben Frey
Photography by Suech + Beck, except family photos courtesy of Trevor Lui
Prop styling by Britt Skelly
Ideation and culinary coordination by Stephanie Lui Valentim
Culinary assistance by Andre Burgos

Editing by Michelle Meade
Copy editing by Judy Phillips
Proofreading by Lucy Kenward
Indexing by Iva Cheung
Narrative text contribution by Randi Bergman

Printed and bound in China by C&C Offset Printing Co., Ltd
Distributed internationally by Publishers Group West

Figure 1 Publishing Inc.
Vancouver BC Canada
www.figure1publishing.com

Recipe Notes

Butter is unsalted unless stated otherwise.

Citrus juices are freshly squeezed.

Eggs are large.

Herbs are fresh unless stated otherwise.

Produce is always medium-sized unless stated otherwise.

Salt is kosher.

Sugar is granulated.

Thank you to our partners who helped
to make this book a reality.

To my parents and grandparents, who paved
the path for my life with love and passion, along
with many other immigrants around the world,
who sacrificed all for the sake of a brighter
day of opportunity for the family.

CON-
TENTS

FOOD SAVED
MY SOUL

There are a few recognizable markers of growing up as a first-generation Canadian: first, you grew up in a household where many of the members didn't speak English. Hell, you might even have been that kid at school who spoke with an accent, even though you were born in Canada. You were also mortified by your "weird" brown-bag lunches (all you ever wanted was a simple peanut butter and jelly sandwich, like everyone else had), yet those so-called weird lunches are exactly what, today, people of all backgrounds crave.

Sound familiar?

Growing up in the suburbs of Toronto, the only son of Chinese immigrants from Hong Kong, I spent much of my time trying to fit into my surroundings. Now my heritage is central to who I am. What's more, it's central to this book and the recipes you'll find here.

The Family Meal

My food journey began in the kitchen of Highbell, the family restaurant my father opened when I was five years old. Like many Chinese restaurants in North America at the time, the menu was a bizarre mix of chow mein, chicken balls, and banquet burgers. It wasn't until I was a teenager that I realized a banquet burger is not, in fact, Chinese food (I'll get to that later). And on a couple of storied occasions, Dad claimed our restaurant to be the first ever "all you can eat" Chinese buffet.

None of it was food that we'd have eaten at home, but it acted as a gateway for burgeoning Chinese food lovers, who could stimulate their palates on deliciously fried dishes and tangy sweet-and-sour sauce.

And hey, it was *damn* good. I still romanticize those chicken balls to this day.

I'd spend a few hours at the restaurant every day after school, watching my grandfather cook up Chinese staples, while my grandmother, the sous chef in charge of the Western menu items, flipped burgers. (I often marvelled at how she, without any culinary training or professional experience, figured out how to skillfully work her way around the grill—not to mention the fryer, stockpots, and cold prep!) My grandfather didn't speak a lick of English, and yet, there he was, watching the hockey game on the TV and hollering at the screen, in Chinglish, *op-side! op-side!* ("offside") as he whipped up the orders.

Once a year, my mother dressed me up in a suit and took me to a fancy restaurant for dinner. She taught me how to open a door for others, pull a chair out from the table for her, and use the proper cutlery for each course. She even taught me how to eat French onion soup the "right" way (that in and of itself is a story). I eventually realized that we could never really afford to do this—the cost of one of these meals was likely equivalent to our week's grocery bill—but my mom felt it was important that I understand and learn these levels of etiquette. I will always be grateful for those meals with her. Because those indulgent dining experiences taught me that how and what we eat should not be bound by class or culture.

I recall going to "Honest Ed" Mirvish's now-defunct Warehouse restaurant so vividly: the fancy chandeliers, the pick forks and many knives, the servers wearing bowties and white gloves. (I discovered

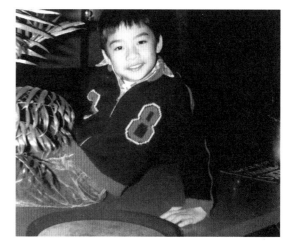

decades later that my grandfather worked the prime-rib cut line there when he first arrived in Canada.) It was opulent, decadent, and so different from our world, but I quickly understood the power a meal has to create both memories and new stories.

I eventually found my own way around a commercial kitchen. By the time I was seven years old, I was on the wok at Highbell, testing out the fiery heat levels and intricate mise en place burner side. The restaurant was like a surrogate babysitter for me.

Each night when it was time for the staff meal, my grandfather would sit down—always in the same chair—fresh off the final service, light his cigarette (back then, one could smoke in restaurants), and observe everyone—from the guests to the staff—enjoying his food. That was my experience of a restaurant family meal.

Memories like these are central to my childhood and form the blueprint of much of my cooking and dining philosophy to this day. Every meal we eat is a story in itself, and while we all have wonderfully rich and textured narratives, we very seldom share them. For some, the warm scent of roasting tomatoes might take them back to Nonna's house. For me, walking into a Chinese noodle shop and smelling congee—Chinese rice porridge (page 154)—takes me right back to Sunday mornings in my mother's kitchen. This book is about those impactful stories and the inspirations along the way that helped shape me and my culinary ambitions and identity.

The Accidental Chef

The last few years have been hugely transformative for me. I spent more than two decades climbing the corporate ladder and achieving the so-called perfect job, working on the food side in hotels, casinos, and convention centres. Through catering banquets and events, I grew into larger roles, with more responsibilities and more success. Yet, despite having a foot in everything, I was always known as the food guy. I spent years trying to shed that moniker before finally realizing, "I *am* the food guy! Why am I fighting this?"

But I didn't want to be the food guy at a convention centre or a casino; I wanted to be the food guy in my own way. I wanted to start my own businesses. I wanted to write my own stories.

I remember the inspiration I got when I chased one of Chef Roy Choi's Kogi trucks in L.A. That brilliant blend of Korean and Mexican flavours all in one bite resonated with me and stuck. So I threw on an apron and got back in the kitchen, behind the bar, and in front of diners. It was a perfect launching point to test out some of my favourite flavours by combining them . . . La Brea was born.

I'd sign up for local weekend pop-ups, show up, and cook. I'd make up dishes as I went along. First, it was Asian empanadas. Then I created Bulgogi Beef Tostadas (page 44) and Guacamame (an edamame guacamole, page 58). I made no money, but I was happier than I'd been in years.

I began to travel more, to meet more people, and to talk more to those in the industry—and that's when my eyes *really* opened. I left the confines of Toronto to explore other Canadian cities—Winnipeg, Calgary, and Halifax. I met Canadians outside my bubble. I visited small towns in Europe and hung out with artisans, chefs, fishermen, and produce vendors and discovered a similarity: that we all held a special part in the food journey, whether we were producing, cooking, or eating. I took a risk by venturing out of my comfort zone and forcing myself to learn at a new level, seeing things through different lenses.

I brought all that knowledge back to Toronto, where I invested in my first restaurant, Kanpai Snack Bar, and helped bring Taiwanese street food to that city, hip hop always blasting from the speakers. The vibe was infectious, and the fried chicken (page 83) was soon voted best in the city by various media outlets. Although I left the venture in 2018, my experiences in that bustling dining room laid the groundwork for culinary ideation.

I was hooked on innovation and, before long, brought the ramen burger (page 102) to the Canadian National Exhibition, a classic summer destination for many Torontonians. I made trips to New York City to research restaurants and food trends, returning to Toronto with ideas of my own. The floodgates were open. And the lineups formed. And just when I thought the response to the snack bar was already crazy, I added the award-winning fried chicken to the already-delicious Last Samurai sandwich, to the shock of the masses.

I think of myself as an accidental chef, much like my grandmother was, slinging those burgers as a new immigrant. I've been in kitchens my entire life and yet, even today, I remain a little gun-shy around classically trained chefs—after all, they've earned themselves the titles of chef. I, on the other hand, am largely self-taught. But I have the business skills from years of building teams and kitchens, and I am as driven and fuelled by my love for food and cooking as they are. Countless hours spent in the kitchen—all that blood, sweat, and tears—eventually paid off and brought me success. I am grateful and humbled in equal measures, and I cannot envision my life being any other way.

In 2017, I had the opportunity to cook for one of the best chefs in the world—Albert Adrià. I was spooked. I thought I didn't deserve to be in the same room as him, and I admired his warmth and curiosity as he peppered me with questions all night. He wanted to learn. Although we are two very different people and two very different cooks, I realized then that we both loved the process of feeding people and conjuring the emotions that comes with it. That inspired me.

In a way, the dining table is one of the few safe spaces we have, one where everyone, regardless of age, socio-economic background, culture, religion, or politics, can come and learn from one another. Some of the coolest chefs and food personalities I've met have contributed recipes to this book (page 168). These talented chefs, culinary advocates, and producers have generously supported me, or their place in this world has impacted my food journey.

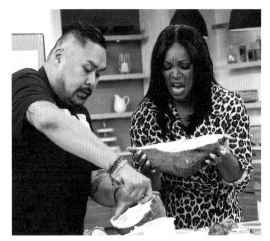

Understanding Our Stories through Food

But back to what I was saying earlier about feeling "other." I'm honoured to be the son of immigrants and to be part of the incredible fabric of Canada. I've never been prouder of my background, both my Chinese heritage and my Toronto upbringing. I live by it and I scream it at the top of my lungs. Food helped me realize this.

I wrote this book in recognition of my parents, grandparents, and all the immigrant families who sacrificed and endured so their kids could grow up to become the people they are today. I know exactly who I am and who I want to be. I'm not there yet, but my experience with the highs and the lows of this industry have helped define me. From random pop-up sessions to late-night cooking in guest kitchens to developing multiple successful (and some not so successful) food brands, I've taken calculated risks, chanced missteps, and at times relied entirely on instinct, all for the sake of feeding people's appetite for memorable experiences. I've moved on from some, maintained others, and have still others on the horizon.

Sometimes I feel like I got to the party late. But people say, "You didn't get to the party late. You just took a left turn."

How to Use This Book

Meals can trigger moments of romanticism or nostalgic soulfulness; they can also help catapult you into the future. All at once, the experience can speak to time, place, and connections. This book is a modern reflection of my journey and all the delectable stories along the way that have shaped who I am today. In fact, my story is probably not too different from yours: special get-togethers, family meals during the holidays, and the random special moments, all stamped with sensory memories that last a lifetime. These are my stories and recipes that I want to share with the world.

This collection of recipes is influenced by my heritage, my restaurants, my family, and my peers. The dishes are fun, accessible, and delicious, and designed for home cooks of all skill levels. Many of the ingredients will be familiar to you and can be found at local supermarkets, but I also want to challenge you to discover some of the lesser known ingredients (page 16). As a chef and food lover, I always feel immense joy when I add a new ingredient or technique to my repertoire.

As a diabetic, I understand the importance of eating to suit the needs of your body. In fact, in my home, stocks are often low-sodium versions, and regular soy sauce is replaced with tamari (a gluten-free soy sauce). For that reason, some recipes in this book are labelled gluten-free (GF), dairy-free (DF), or vegetarian (VEG)—so you know at a glance if they meet your dietary requirements. And for some recipes, I've included a tip on how to adapt it to suit a certain dietary need.

As mentioned, I have included personal stories of experiences that have shaped me and my culinary identity. These "Soulful Food Stories," found between the chapters, highlight recipes that have impacted those moments in my life. While they are simple expressions of my own life story, I hope they will entertain, resonate, or inspire you to make valuable connections with your own memories and soulful food stories. I'd love to hear about them someday. See you in the kitchen and at the dining table.

MY KITCHEN PLAYLIST:
HIP HOP HOORAY

Often blaring in the dining rooms and kitchens of some of the best eateries, hip hop has an interesting connection to food. This particular music genre has helped shape my life and inform the dining experiences at my restaurants. Here are a few of the classics, a soundtrack of my world, call it my "life's mix tape". . . Parental Guidance Advised.

Fight the Power
Public Enemy

Scenario
A Tribe Called Quest

Me Myself and I
De La Soul

N.Y. State of Mind
Nas

Juicy
The Notorious B.I.G.

Rebirth of Slick
Digable Planets

**They Reminisce
Over You**
Pete Rock & CL Smooth

You Gots to Chill
EPMD

C.R.E.A.M
Wu-Tang Clan

Headlines
Drake

Treat 'Em Right
Chubb Rock

Double Up
Nipsey Hussle

It's a Shame (My Sister)
Monie Love

Family and Loyalty
Gang Starr

The Boomin' System
by LL Cool J

Passin Me By
The Pharcyde

It Was A Good Day
Ice Cube

People Everyday
Arrested Development

IT'S MY THING
(PANTRY ESSENTIALS)

We are surrounded by international flavours and cultural influences, and my adventurous palate is always ready to have its boundaries pushed. These essential ingredients rekindle the flavours of my journey and glam up ordinary dishes into delicious and soulful memories. They also make my life in the kitchen that much easier and tastier. I encourage you to stock up on your favourites; most can be found at large grocers, specialty shops, and ethnic markets.

adobo chipotle Chipotles—dried smoked jalapeños—are canned in a tangy, slightly sweet red sauce. They add a deep sour-sweet smoky chile heat to dishes that's so good, Drake even wrote a song about it ("0 to 100/The Catch Up").

agave nectar The word "nectar" is actually redundant given that agave is the sweet syrup derived from the fluid of the blue agave plant. Commonly used by diabetics because of its low glycemic index, this all-natural, plant-derived sweetener should be used sparingly, as it's a sugar nonetheless. It is also commercially used to produce tequila.

canola oil Canola oil, a vegetable oil derived from a certain variety of rapeseed, is generally regarded as a healthy oil because it is so low in saturated fat. But I enjoy cooking with it for its neutral flavour and high smoke point (it's amazing for flash-frying) and because it's 100% Canadian.

chiles Beyond adding heat, chiles can suffuse a dish with layers of flavours. They are incredibly versatile: fresh, smoked, or dehydrated, they can be added to marinades and stir-fries, and used as garnish.

I mainly use three types. The *bird's eye chile* may be small but packs a lot of heat. The *serrano pepper* hails from the mountainous regions of the Mexican states of Puebla and Hidalgo. While it is milder than a bird's eye chile, it can make for a good substitute. The *jalapeño* is dark green, thick-fleshed, and slightly sweet (and turns red when fully ripe). It has a medium heat with fresh, grassy notes.

Take care when handling chiles—you might want to wear gloves when cutting them, and don't touch your face or eyes after handling. Wash your hands, knife, and cutting board well afterward. Beware of the fumes of dried chiles wafting into your eyes when processing them.

chili oil Chili oil is a popular seasoning and condiment in Chinese cooking. Typically red, it consists of oil (often vegetable, soybean, or sesame) enhanced with red chile peppers, Sichuan peppercorns, spices, ginger, and toasted sesame seeds. It is sometimes used as a condiment for meat and dim sum. It is also used in the Korean Chinese noodle soup dish *jjamppong*. I sometimes blend the oil with other chiles or chili condiments.

chili paste Asian chile pastes are indispensable to my everyday cooking. These hot sauces are generally made with ground chiles, oil, vinegar, and salt, but they can also be enhanced with other flavours, such as garlic, ginger, sugar, sesame, black beans, or fermented soybeans. The most recognizable chili pastes include Sriracha (*see also* Sriracha) and, though perhaps less so, gochujang paste (*see also* gochujang paste).

Chinese black vinegar This aged vinegar from the Chinese province of Chinkiang is typically derived from glutinous rice and malt. With its deep black colour and mild sharpness, it is similar to balsamic vinegar. I use it in marinades, stir-fries, braises, and dipping sauces.

Chinese cooking wine (*Shaoxing*) Arguably as important as soy sauce when it comes to Chinese cooking, this fermented rice wine has a harsh salty, alcoholic flavour (don't go drinking it!) that can mask other flavours, so use it sparingly. I love using it in slow-cooked braised meat dishes, Stephanie's Mooshie Mooshie (page 110), Chicken and Mushroom Stir-Fry (page 126), and Honey-Garlic Spare Ribs (page 132).

Chinese sausage (*lap cheong*) "Chinese sausage" is an overarching term used to describe various types of sausages available in China; my favourite is the Hong Kong–style *lap cheong*. This dried, hard, pork-based sausage, often smoked, sweetened, and seasoned, can be used in a traditional turnip cake (page 34) and Asian-inspired tapas (page 30). Some families will even add sliced lap cheong to a rice cooker, to impart its delicious flavour to the rice.

coconut milk Great for South Asian–style dishes, coconut milk adds richness and fragrance to curries and desserts alike. It also makes for a great dairy-free alternative to milk.

cornstarch I often use cornstarch as a thickener for sauces, though it also makes for a good dredge for frying meats (which helps the meat brown and keep it juicy inside).

doubanjiang paste This salty paste—made from fermented broad beans, soybeans, salt, rice, and spices—is the soul of Sichuan cooking. Also known as fermented chili broad bean paste, it brings a bold flavour to dishes such as Mapo Tofu (page 131). It comes in both regular and spicy versions, and I prefer the type that is wrapped in a kraft paper bag.

dried mushrooms Dried mushrooms have intense flavour. Dried *porcini* are most commonly used in Western dishes, but my recipes wouldn't be the same without dried *shiitakes* and *wood ear* mushrooms. Be sure to rinse dried mushrooms, then soak them in warm water for 1–1½ hours to hydrate before using.

dried scallops Dried scallops, or conpoy, have a distinct smell—marine, pungent, and reminiscent of certain salt-cured meats. They add a rich umami taste to dishes.

fish sauce Fish sauce is a fermented fish condiment commonly used in East and South Asia. Sweet, salty, fishy, and pungent, it is used sparingly to flavour stir-fries, stews, and soups. It's also used as a salt replacement.

five-spice powder Five-spice powder is a beautifully warm and aromatic spice mixture of star anise, cloves, Chinese cinnamon, Sichuan pepper, and fennel seeds.

adobo chipotle

agave nectar

chili paste

Chinese black vinegar

chili oil

canola oil

chiles

Chinese cooking wine (Shaoxing)

doubanjiang paste

Chinese sausage (lap cheong)

five-spice powder

coconut milk

furikake

dried mushrooms

fish sauce

hoisin
sauce

mirin

oyster sauce

rice vinegar

gochujang paste

preserved mustard greens

nori

sambal oelek

kimchi

sweet
chili
sauce

sweet
soy
sauce

tamari

miso paste

Sriracha

togarashi

furikake Furikake is a dry Japanese seasoning made of bonito, sesame seeds, and toasted seaweed that can be sprinkled over cooked rice, vegetables, or fish.

gochujang paste Gochujang paste, a Korean chile paste made with glutinous rice and fermented soybeans, is all at once savoury, sweet, and spicy (some refer to this as the ketchup of Korea). This thick, sticky condiment also has a concentrated, pungent flavour that works particularly well in Udon-Stuffed Meatballs (page 32).

hoisin sauce Commonly used as a meat glaze, a seasoning for stir-fries, or a dipping sauce, this thick, fragrant, nearly black sauce has a robust sweet and salty flavour. Some brands produce a gluten-free version.

kimchi A staple Korean side dish of salted and fermented vegetables generally including napa cabbage, radishes, and sometimes pear or apple. Personally, I love it and use it to complement many things from scrambled eggs to sandwiches.

mirin Mirin is a sweet, tangy Japanese rice wine—think teriyaki sauce. A staple in Japanese cooking, it's used as both as a seasoning and a glaze.

miso paste This essential Japanese seasoning is made with fermenting soybeans, koji, salt, and, on some occasions, rice, barley, and seaweed. The basis of miso soup, it also adds savoury umami to vinaigrettes (page 50).

nori You've seen nori used to wrap sushi rolls and onigiri, but it can also be added to ramen (page 164) or shredded to make a tasty topping for rice or noodle dishes (page 163).

oyster sauce Even though this delicious dark sauce is made from boiled oysters, there's nothing fishy about it. Instead, its unique complex salty and sweet flavour is loaded with umami.

pepper, black and white Both black and white peppercorns are the fruit of the pepper plant, but they have different flavour profiles because they are processed differently. Black peppercorns are picked when almost ripe and then sun-dried, which turns the outer layer black. With white peppercorns, the outer layer is removed either pre- or post- drying. White peppercorns are hotter than black but have fewer flavour notes. I use both in equal measure, but I couldn't live without white pepper to season my favourite fried chicken recipes.

preserved mustard greens Preserved mustard greens, also known in Cantonese as *mui choy*, are preserved with salt and sugar. They are available dried, or hydrated in a vacuum-packed bag.

rice vinegar Rice vinegar is sweet and mild used in Japanese cooking. It's a main ingredient in sushi rice but also provides great flavour and balance to dressings.

rock sugar Rock sugar, sometimes called rock candy or sugar candy, is available as irregular lumps of crystallized, refined sugar. Opaque and gold, it has a clean taste and is less sweet than granulated sugar.

sambal oelek This Indonesian chili sauce or paste is typically made with various chile peppers, shrimp paste, garlic, ginger, shallot, spring onions, palm sugar, and lime juice. My Durty Fries (page 28) and Salted Fried Chicken Wings (page 84) aren't the same without it.

sesame oil Sesame oil is derived from sesame seeds. It can be used as a cooking oil, though its nutty aroma and taste make for a great flavour enhancer—just be sure to use it sparingly, as it's strong-tasting and could overpower the dish.

sesame seeds I often finish a dish with sesame seeds to add colour, texture, and nuttiness. Sesame seeds come in white, black, and even a "tuxedo" blend, which is a combination of the two.

shiitake mushrooms (see dried mushrooms)

soy sauce The holy elixir of Chinese cooking. This liquid gold is made from a fermented paste of soybeans, salt, water, and sometimes roasted grains. As a diabetic who needs to be mindful of my glycemic index, I often replace regular soy sauce with a gluten-free substitute called tamari (*see also* tamari).

Sriracha This essential hot sauce is a favourite among chefs and heat seekers alike. It's made with chile peppers, distilled vinegar, garlic, sugar, and salt, and I can't think of a more versatile condiment that works with the foods of so many cultures. Fun fact: it's so popular that the Huy Fong Foods company manufactures 3,000 bottles an hour. (That's fifty bottles every second!)

sweet chili sauce Also known as Thai sweet chili sauce or Asian sweet chili sauce, this highly delicious condiment boasts sweet, savoury, zingy, and spicy notes. It can be served on the side as a dipping sauce, especially for cauliflower wings (page 57) or fried chicken (page 83).

sweet soy sauce Sweet soy sauce, a dark and syrupy Indonesian condiment, has a flavour not unlike molasses (courtesy of the addition of palm sugar). Also known as *kecap manis,* it is widely used with satay and common Hong Kong–style dishes like *cheung fun* and clay pot rice.

tamari (gluten-free soy) Tamari (or *tamari shoyu*) is a Japanese condiment made of fermented soybeans. Thicker and more balanced in flavour than regular soy sauce, it is a good vegan-friendly and gluten-free substitute.

togarashi Also known as *shichimi,* this popular Japanese spice mixture is prepared with chili powder, seaweed, orange zest, ginger, and sesame seeds.

街頭小食

STREET SNACKS

ANEETA'S SIMPLE SICILIAN

My wife, Aneeta, and I first experienced this five-bite sandwich at a small roadside café on our first trip to Palermo, Sicily. For me, many of the Italian bread dishes bring to mind Hong Kong–style bakeries, with their endless rows of brioche. This is a romanticized version of a classic Chinese café bun, served with a fuss-free tomato-basil salad. It amazes me that something so simple can be so delicious.

Spread butter on cut sides of buns. Layer 2–3 slices of mortadella on each bun bottom. Top with the bun top.

For the salad, layer tomatoes on a plate, then drizzle with oil. Garnish with basil and season with salt and pepper.

The Message Traditionally, this sandwich calls for regular mortadella, but I love the mild heat of spicy mortadella. Be sure to choose the regular cut, not the lean variety, as the fattiness is key here. And have your butcher slice it wafer thin.

Serves 6 (as snacks)

QUICK
Prep 10 min

3 Tbsp salted butter
6 fresh-baked mini brioche buns, halved
3½ oz spicy mortadella, thinly sliced (see note)
3 Roma tomatoes, thinly sliced
3 Tbsp extra-virgin olive oil
3–4 basil leaves, cut into thin strips
Pinch of salt
Pinch of black pepper

CORN AND CHORIZO SOPAS

When the team and I relaunched the pop-up La Brea at Toronto's Stackt Market (the largest shipping-container market in Canada), it was on the heels of the fall season. Realizing Canadians' love of soup, I wanted to riff on a Chinese classic, cream of corn soup. To give it a Latin feel, we added chorizo and topped it with fresh, herbaceous cilantro and a squeeze of fresh lime.

Heat oil in a saucepan over high heat. Add chorizo and cook for 2 minutes. Stir in corn and sauté for 3–4 minutes. Pour in stock, reduce heat to medium-low, and simmer the soup for 10 minutes.

Crack eggs into a small bowl. Gently add eggs to soup and, using a long spoon or spatula, immediately whisk soup to break down the eggs. Add dried cilantro, salt, and pepper. Simmer for 12–15 minutes on low heat.

Ladle soup into bowls and garnish with crispy shallots, cilantro, and a lime wedge.

Serves 2–4

DF, GF, QUICK
Prep 10 min
Cook 20–25 min

1 Tbsp canola oil
3½ oz Mexican chorizo, cooked and chopped
½ cup corn kernels
2 cups vegetable stock
2 eggs
½ tsp dried cilantro
½ tsp salt
½ tsp black pepper
Crispy shallots, for garnish
Cilantro, for garnish
Lime wedges, for garnish

CHIPS WITH THE DIP: THE LARRY O.B.

This creation sees a combination of La Brea flavours and international ingredients—tortilla chips, bulgogi beef, queso fresco, cotija cheese, spring onions, and kimchi—layered together to create a nacho ode to Toronto's first NBA basketball championship. This is the ultimate "chips with the dip."

Lime crema Combine all ingredients in a bowl. Refrigerate until needed.

Chips Heat oil in a medium saucepan over high heat to a temperature of 400°F. Gently lower in tortillas, using a metal slotted spoon or spider and working in batches to avoid overcrowding, and deep-fry for 4–5 minutes, until crisp and golden. Transfer to a plate lined with paper towel to drain, then season with salt.

Combine Sriracha and honey in a small bowl.

Spread out half the tortilla chips on a large platter. Drizzle half with the lime crema, then with the Sriracha mixture. Garnish with half the spring onions, half the kimchi, and half of both cheeses. Create a second layer with the remaining chips and top with bulgogi beef. Scatter remaining kimchi overtop, then drizzle with the lime crema and the Sriracha mixture. Scatter with the remaining cheeses and spring onions, and crispy shallots. Garnish with cilantro.

Serve with guacamame, salsa picante, and lime wedges.

Make It Gluten-Free This dish can be made gluten-free by using tamari instead of soy sauce.

Serves 2–4

QUICK
Prep 10 min
Cook 25 min

Lime crema
½ cup sour cream
Juice of 1 lime
Salt and black pepper
    to taste

Chips
2½ cups canola oil
10 (5-inch) corn tortillas,
    each cut into 6 equal wedges
Salt to taste
3 Tbsp Sriracha
1 Tbsp local honey
2 spring onions, chopped
⅓ cup finely chopped kimchi
¼ cup crumbled queso fresco
¼ cup crumbled cotija cheese
5 oz Bulgogi Beef (page 44)
1 Tbsp crispy shallots
¼ cup coarsely chopped
    cilantro, for garnish
½ cup Guacamame (page 58),
    to serve
Salsa picante, to serve
2 lime wedges, to serve

DURTY FRIES

Sometimes the best recipes are happy accidents. When creating a Japanese-inspired menu at Yatai to accompany our ramen burger, the fries had to make the cut. It was an exercise in creativity, combining seemingly random ingredients from the pantry, but we hit the jackpot. This tasty dish has been revived and is now a bestseller at Joybird Fried Chicken & Side Things. I recommend serving it with The Last Samurai (page 102) or The Highbell Banquet Burger (page 100).

Put potatoes in a bowl of cold water and set aside.

Melt butter in a small saucepan over medium-high heat. Add teriyaki sauce and bring to a simmer. Reduce heat to low and cook for another 5 minutes. Remove from heat.

Heat oil in a deep fryer or deep saucepan to a temperature of 365°F. Drain potatoes, then pat dry. Using a metal slotted spoon, carefully lower potatoes into the oil, working in batches if necessary to avoid overcrowding, and deep-fry for 7–8 minutes, until golden and edges are slightly crispy. (If they are golden brown, they have been in the oil too long.) Turn off heat, then transfer fries to a plate lined with paper towel to drain and let cool.

In a small bowl, combine Kewpie (or mayonnaise), sambal, and Sriracha.

Reheat oil to a temperature of 350°F. Return fries to the oil and "double-fry" for another 3–4 minutes, until golden brown. Using a metal slotted spoon, drain and transfer fries to a mixing bowl.

Immediately pour in teriyaki butter and toss the fries to coat. Season with furikake, salt, and pepper and toss fries again to coat. Transfer fries to a serving bowl or basket, drizzle with Sriracha mayo, and garnish with spring onions.

Serves 4

VEG
Prep 10 min
Cook 30 min

5 russet potatoes, peeled and cut into 3-inch-long batons
¼ cup (½ stick) butter
¼ cup teriyaki sauce
4–5 cups canola oil
3 Tbsp Kewpie or regular mayonnaise
½ tsp sambal oelek
½ tsp Sriracha
1 tsp furikake
½ tsp salt
¼ tsp black pepper
1 spring onion, chopped

Make It Gluten-Free
This dish can be made gluten-free by using a gluten-free version of teriyaki sauce.

MOM'S EASY WONTONS

In so many cultures, making dumplings at home is a familial pastime. For us Chinese, wontons are eaten at restaurants (and served in our own home), and are also a part of our kitchen traditions at home. My mom taught me how to make them and, years later, I make them with my daughter, too. This is a spin on Mom's dumplings, served with a simple dipping sauce.

Dipping sauce Combine all ingredients in a small bowl.

Wontons In a bowl, combine pork, shrimp, spring onions, and ginger. Season with salt and pepper.

Fill a small bowl with water. Place a teaspoon of filling in the centre of a wrapper. Using your fingertips, grab all corners of wrapper and bunch together (like a little purse bundle). Dab with water and press to seal. (Ensure the dumplings are sealed. To seal any holes, dab water along the edge, then press sides together.) Place on a lightly floured baking sheet and repeat with the remaining filling and wrappers.

Bring a medium saucepan of water to a boil. Reduce heat to medium-low and simmer. Using a metal slotted spoon, gently lower 8–10 wontons into water and cook for 5–7 minutes, until they float to the surface. Transfer wontons to a shallow bowl. Repeat with the remaining batches.

Divide wontons among 4 bowls and pour 1 cup stock into each. Garnish with spring onions and serve with dipping sauce.

Serves 4

DF
Prep 20 min
Cook 15–25 min

Dipping sauce
3 Tbsp soy sauce or tamari
½ tsp sesame oil
½ tsp chili oil
½ tsp rice wine vinegar

Wontons
8 oz ground pork
8 oz shrimp, shelled, deveined, and finely chopped
1 spring onion, finely chopped, plus extra for garnish
2 tsp finely chopped ginger
Salt and black pepper to taste
24 square wonton wrappers
All-purpose flour, for dusting
4 cups hot vegetable or chicken stock

CHINESE SAUSAGE CROQUETAS

In 2016, I took part in an Estrella Damm Gastronomic Experience in Barcelona (along with *the* iconic Michelin star chef Ferran Adrià, page 178). This was our creation for the event. Fast-forward two years and I am welcoming Albert and his team to our Taiwanese snack bar in Toronto. Little did I know that he is a fan of Asian cuisine and wanted to dine with us. Food allows us to cross cultural boundaries, providing us with new culinary experiences.

Preheat oven to 325°F. Brush bell pepper with olive oil and season with salt and pepper. Roast for 15–20 minutes, until pepper is softened and cooked through.

Put potatoes in a stockpot, add enough cold water to cover, and bring to a boil. Cook for 12–15 minutes, until tender. Drain. In a mixing bowl, combine milk, butter, ½ teaspoon salt, and ⅓ teaspoon pepper. Add potatoes and mash until smooth. Set aside to cool, then stir in Chinese sausage and onions.

In a food processor, process roasted pepper, mayonnaise, chili oil, and lemon juice until smooth. Transfer the aioli to a bowl, cover, and refrigerate for 1½ to 2 hours.

Take ¼ cup potato mixture in your hands and shape into a 3½-inch torpedo-shaped croquette. Repeat until all the mixture is used. Pour eggs into a shallow bowl. Place breadcrumbs in another. Coat each croqueta in egg, then in the breadcrumbs. Collect them on a baking sheet.

Heat oil in a deep fryer or deep saucepan over high heat to 375°F. Add croquetas and deep-fry for 8–10 minutes, until they are golden brown and float to the surface. Using a metal slotted spoon, transfer to a plate lined with paper towel to drain. Sprinkle with smoked salt and garnish with parsley, then serve with roasted red pepper aioli.

Serves 4

Prep 20 min, plus 1½–2 hr chilling time
Cook 30 min

½ red bell pepper
2 Tbsp olive oil
Salt and black pepper
3 russet potatoes, peeled and cut into 1½-inch cubes
¼ cup 2% milk
2 Tbsp melted butter
2 Chinese sausages, finely chopped
½ onion, finely chopped
½ cup mayonnaise
1 Tbsp chili oil
Juice of ½ lemon
2 eggs, beaten
2 cups panko breadcrumbs
Canola oil, for frying
Smoked salt, for garnish
Sprig of Italian parsley, finely chopped, for garnish

Make It Gluten-Free
This dish can be made gluten-free by using gluten-free panko breadcrumbs.

UDON-STUFFED MEATBALLS

When I worked with Xbox on the launch of its *Gears of War* video game series, I was challenged to create dishes that took the form of game scenes or montages. These delicious, albeit gory, meatballs were presented at an exclusive VIP dinner and, later, at my fried chicken stand, which was converted for the day into a video game pop-up venue. Then, I called this bestselling meatball "Mutated Serapede Sac, Riftworm Noodles in Blood Gochujang," but I've opted for something much simpler (and hopefully more appealing!) for this book.

Bring a saucepan of water to a boil. Add udon and cook for 2–3 minutes, stirring occasionally to separate noodles. Drain, then set aside in a bowl.

Heat oil in a small saucepan over low heat. Add gochujang and lightly stir. Stir in noodles and sugar. Add 1½ tablespoons water.

In a small bowl, combine cornstarch and 1½ tablespoons water. Pour mixture into the pan and cook until sauce has thickened. (If sauce is too thick, add a little more water.)

Remove pan from heat and let stand for 20 minutes, until noodles are fully cooled. Compact noodles into 4 balls of equal size. (Because the noodles are thick, they may require some effort to shape.)

Preheat oven to 375°F. Grease a small baking sheet.

In a mixing bowl, combine pork, beef, onions, cilantro, togarashi, and bulgogi marinade. Press pork mixture over noodle balls until completely covered. Season with togarashi if desired.

Place meatballs on the prepared baking sheet and bake for 30–35 minutes, until surface is golden brown and slightly caramelized. Remove from oven and let rest for 3–5 minutes.

Set a meatball in the centre of each plate. With a spoon, drizzle gochujang sauce over the noodles.

Serves 4 (as an appetizer)

DF
Prep 15 min,
plus 20 min cooling time
Cook 55 min

7½ oz uncooked
   udon noodles
1½ Tbsp canola oil,
   plus extra for greasing
3 Tbsp gochujang paste
1½ tsp brown sugar
1 tsp cornstarch
7 oz ground pork
7 oz *Certifed Angus Beef*
   lean ground chuck
3 Tbsp finely chopped red onion
½ tsp dried cilantro
½ tsp togarashi,
   plus extra to taste
2 Tbsp Bulgogi Beef marinade
   (page 44)

BLACK BEAN CHICKEN TACO

The American west coast is a great inspiration when it comes to food ideas. It was on a trip to Los Angeles that I heard about Roy Choi's Kogi BBQ Taco truck, which was sending location updates only via Twitter. Naturally, I spent a day following the truck around the city. His unique take on a Korean taco was one reason La Brea eventually took form: I discovered how Asian and Latin flavours can come together so beautifully in a simple dish. Here, I've married the classic Chinese dish of black bean chicken with a corn tortilla and fresh garnishes.

Chicken filling In a bowl, combine black bean sauce, garlic, soy sauce (or tamari), and sugar. Add chicken to the marinade, stirring to coat. Cover and refrigerate for 1 hour.

Slaw Place all ingredients in a small bowl, tossing to mix. Set aside.

Lime crema In a small bowl, combine all ingredients. Refrigerate until needed.

Assembly Heat oil in a frying pan over high heat. Add chicken filling, reduce heat to medium-high, and cook for 8 minutes, stirring constantly, until cooked through. Cover and remove from heat.

In a dry frying pan over medium heat, add a tortilla and warm each side for 1 minute. Repeat with the remaining tortillas; keep warm.

Place a tortilla on a plate. Place some slaw in the centre, add a spoonful of chicken, and top with a dollop of lime crema. Top with spring onions, sesame seeds, crispy garlic flakes, and cilantro. Serve immediately.

The Message Asian stores sell dried garlic flakes in bags or jars. If you prefer, use Crispy Garlic Chips (page 132) instead.

Make It Gluten-Free This dish can be made gluten-free by using tamari instead of soy sauce.

Makes 8

Prep 15 min, plus
1 hr marinating time
Cook 25 min

Chicken filling
1 Tbsp black bean sauce
  (such as Lee Kum Kee)
1 clove garlic, finely chopped
½ tsp soy sauce or tamari
¼ tsp sugar
3 skinless, boneless chicken
  thighs, cut into bite-sized
  pieces

Slaw
½ cup shredded green cabbage
1 carrot, shredded
3 Tbsp apple cider vinegar
1½ Tbsp canola oil
½ tsp sugar
¼ tsp salt

Lime crema
¼ cup sour cream
Juice of ½ lime
Salt and black pepper to taste

Assembly
1 Tbsp canola oil
Chicken Filling (see here)
8 (4-inch) corn tortillas
Slaw (see here)
Lime Crema (see here)
1 spring onion, finely chopped
1 Tbsp sesame seeds, toasted
1 Tbsp crispy garlic flakes
  (see note)
2 sprigs cilantro, hand torn

XO TURNIP CAKE
(LO BOK GO)

Turnip cake is a traditional Chinese dish often served at dim sum. (Curiously, the recipe doesn't actually feature any turnip but, rather, daikon, a type of radish.) My maternal grandma, affectionately known as *po po*, prepared this for special occasions. The recipe varies from family to family, but I love her version when pan-fried crispy on the outside. My interpretation has been wok-fried with spicy and savoury XO hot sauce.

Place mushrooms, dried scallops, and 1 cup hot water in a bowl and soak for 1½ hours, until fully hydrated.

Coarsely grate half of the daikon. Cut the other half into ¼-inch cubes.

Reserve mushroom-scallop soaking liquid. Remove mushroom stems and finely chop. Using your fingers, tear scallops apart.

Heat 1 teaspoon oil in a large saucepan over medium-high heat. Add Chinese sausage and cook for 3–4 minutes, until fat is rendered. Add scallops and mushrooms and sauté for 2–3 minutes. Stir in all the daikon and the mushroom-scallop soaking liquid. Simmer for 5 minutes, then reduce heat to medium and cook for 3–4 minutes, until daikon is soft and translucent. Strain through a colander, reserving the liquid. Transfer daikon to a large bowl and set both the daikon and reserved cooking liquid aside to cool.

In a small bowl, combine rice flour, cornstarch, salt, pepper, and sugar. Pour in soy sauce (or tamari) and 1 cup reserved cooking liquid and mix until smooth. Pour mixture into the bowl with the daikon, add half of the spring onions, and mix well.

Heat 1 tablespoon oil in the same pan over medium heat. Add daikon mixture, then reduce heat to low. Fold contents for 4–5 minutes, allowing mixture to thicken to a paste. Remove pan from heat.

Serves 4

DF
Prep 15 min, plus 1½ hr hydrating time
Cook 1¼ hr

5 dried shiitake mushrooms, rinsed
2–4 dried scallops (conpoy), rinsed
1 (1-lb) daikon radish (divided)
6½ tsp canola oil (divided)
2 Chinese sausage, finely chopped
⅔ cup rice flour
1 tsp cornstarch
1 tsp salt
½ tsp white pepper
½ tsp sugar
1 tsp soy sauce or tamari
2 spring onions, chopped (divided)
2 Tbsp XO sauce
Chili oil or chili paste, to serve

Make It Gluten-Free This dish can be made gluten-free by using tamari instead of soy sauce.

Pour mixture into a deep disposable round or rectangular (approximately 2- × 9-inch) foil pan that will fit in a large steamer basket.

Fill water to the highest level in a steamer and bring to a boil. Place foil pan in the steamer basket, cover, and steam cake for 50 minutes, until cooked through (when a chopstick or toothpick is inserted into the centre and comes out clean).

Allow turnip cake to cool to room temperature. Cover and refrigerate until firm, about 8 hours.

Remove cake from pan by running a knife around the edge of the pan, then inverting cake onto a cutting board. Cut into 2-inch cubes.

Heat the remaining 1½ teaspoons oil in a frying pan over high heat. Add turnip cake and sear for 5–6 minutes, tossing in the pan occasionally. Reduce heat to medium. Add XO sauce and toss to coat evenly, then transfer to a serving platter. Garnish with the remaining spring onions. Serve with a side of chili oil or paste.

TAIWANESE BAR SNACKS

Whereas, in North American bars, you'll find mixed nuts or snack mixes, in Taiwanese establishments, you'll find salty, savoury dried fish. We introduced this recipe to Torontonians at Kanpai—naturally, some people had reservations about eating dried fish, but once they tried it, they always came back for more.

Place sardines in a bowl and cover with warm water. Cover bowl and let sardines rehydrate for at least 8 hours.

Heat oil in a wok or frying pan over high heat. Drain sardines, then add to the pan and sauté for 2–3 minutes. Add spring onions, chiles, and tofu and sauté for 2 minutes, until sardines begin to crisp. Reduce heat to medium and add soy sauce (or tamari). Stir in peanuts, season with salt and pepper, and toss to mix.

Transfer to a serving platter and serve immediately.

The Message Japanese dried baby sardines, known as *niboshi*, are used throughout Asia either as snacks or as seasoning for soup stocks and other dishes. Commonly referred to as anchovies, they can be found at Asian grocery stores.

Make It Gluten-Free This dish can be made gluten-free by using tamari instead of soy sauce.

Serves 2

DF
Prep 5 min
plus 8 hr soaking time
Cook 5 min

1 cup Japanese dried sardines (see note)
2 Tbsp canola oil
3 spring onions, chopped (½ cup)
1 bird's eye chile, finely chopped
½ cup marinated tofu, cut into thin strips
2 tsp soy sauce or tamari
¼ cup unsalted roasted peanuts
Salt and black pepper to taste

GARNISHES AND TOPPINGS (THIS IS HOW WE DO IT)

Like the accoutrements of the perfect outfit, garnishes bring that final accent to a dish. Not only do they enhance the appearance and presentation of the food, they also bring bursts of colour, texture, and balance. Best of all, you probably already stock some of the best garnishes in your pantry or refrigerator.

Once I've established the basis of a dish, garnishes help me fill in the blanks—I ask myself whether the dish is balanced, needs crunchy texture, or has enough colour to appeal. I arrange, whether on the countertop or the dining table, the garnishes neatly by category—crunch, freshness, heat, acidity, and so on—so that I can navigate my options quickly and efficiently.

You can choose from one or several garnishes, but either way, I encourage you to take risks to make flavour discoveries. The process rarely disappoints.

Acid
Lemon
Lime
Pickled jalapeños
Pickled peppers
Pickled lo bok (daikon)

Crunch
Crispy lentils
Crispy proteins (lardons, bacon bits, chicharron, chicken skin)
Fried garlic
Fried onions
Fried shallots
Nuts
Roasted chickpeas
Slaw

Fresh Greens
Amaranth
Cilantro
Micro greens
Parsley
Sorrel
Spring onions

Heat
Chiles (fresh and dried)
Hot sauce

Richness
Cheese (grated)
Cream/crema
Tahini
Yogurt

Sauce
Gochujang paste
Hoisin sauce
Ponzu
Sriracha
Vinegars

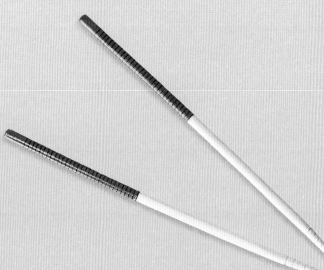

TAIPEI CEVICHE WITH TARO CRISPS

Inspired by esteemed chefs Ferran and Albert Adrià, who were involved—together with Estrella Damm, the beer of Barcelona—with culinary congresses that push the boundaries of tapas, this dish was conceived as a special offering for a city-wide event in Toronto where we offered unique tapas in our Taiwanese restaurant. Micro daikon can be found at produce stores or fine grocers.

Drain and pat dry shrimp, then place in a bowl. Add squid, apples, bell peppers, Thai basil, chiles, and cilantro. Add citrus juices, oil, ¼ teaspoon salt, pepper, and lime zest and mix well. Cover and refrigerate ceviche for at least 8 hours.

Using a mandolin (use the guard!), shave taro into thin slices and soak in water for 5 minutes. Drain and pat dry.

Heat oil in a deep saucepan over high heat. Using a metal slotted spoon, gently lower taro into the oil and deep-fry for 3–4 minutes, until they are golden brown and float to the surface. Transfer to a plate lined with paper towel to drain. Season with the remaining ¼ teaspoon salt.

Transfer ceviche to a serving bowl, garnish with micro daikon, and serve with taro crisps.

Serves 2–4

DF, GF
Prep 15 min, plus 8 hr marinating time
Cook 5 min

8 (26/30) raw shrimp, shelled, deveined, and finely chopped
1 small fresh squid body, cleaned and finely chopped
¼ Fuji apple, unpeeled, cored, and finely chopped
¼ red bell pepper, seeded, deveined, and finely chopped
4–5 Thai basil leaves, finely chopped
½ bird's eye chile, seeded, deveined, and finely chopped
Sprig of cilantro, finely chopped
Juice of 1½ limes, plus a pinch of grated zest
Juice of ½ lemon
1 tsp canola oil, plus extra for deep-frying
½ tsp salt (divided)
¼ tsp black pepper
4 oz taro root, peeled and washed
Micro daikon, for garnish

MC LYTE BAO

When we launched the Taiwanese snack bar, we got in at the top end of the bao craze. Bao are Chinese stuffed and steamed wheat buns, and our classic *guo bao* and fried chicken versions were always a hit, but surprisingly—for us at least—so was our vegetarian option. We were so humbled by its inclusion in a *Toronto Life* write-up of the best sandwiches in the city, and it fills me with pride to share it with you here. Lighter than its pork belly and fried chicken counterparts (but equally substantial!), the name pays homage to one of the great original female hip-hop MCs of my generation.

Slaw Place all ingredients in a bowl, tossing to mix well. Cover and refrigerate for at least 8 hours.

Pickles Place all ingredients in a small bowl, tossing to mix well. Cover and refrigerate for at least 8 hours.

Sauce Combine all ingredients in a small bowl. Refrigerate until needed.

Batter In a mixing bowl, combine all ingredients and ½ cup water and mix until smooth.

DF, VEG
Prep 10 min, plus 8 hr marinating time
Cook 15 min

Slaw
1½ cups shredded purple cabbage
1 Tbsp apple cider vinegar
1 tsp canola oil
½ tsp salt
½ tsp sugar
Black pepper to taste

Pickles
12 thin rounds cucumber
1 star anise
¼ cup white vinegar
1½ Tbsp sugar
1 tsp pickling spice
1 tsp salt

Sauce
⅓ cup mayonnaise
1 Tbsp finely chopped preserved mustard greens
1 tsp Sriracha
½ tsp local honey or agave nectar

Batter
⅓ cup tapioca starch
2 tsp cornstarch
2 tsp custard powder (such as Bird's)
⅓ tsp black pepper

Assembly Drain slaw and pickles.

Heat oil in a deep saucepan over high heat. Dip the sweet potatoes in the batter, coating them completely, then, using a metal slotted spoon, carefully lower them into the oil and deep-fry for 3–4 minutes, until they float to the surface. Transfer to a plate lined with paper towel to drain. Season with salt. Keep warm and crisp in the oven on low heat.

Line a steamer with parchment paper and, using a fork or knife, pierce a few holes in the paper. Lay bao flat, spaced apart, and steam for 7–8 minutes, until fluffy.

Place 2 slices of sweet potato on the bottom half of a bao. Top with slaw, a drizzle of sauce, pickles, and cilantro. If needed, use bamboo skewers to hold bao together.

Assembly
Slaw (see here)
Pickles (see here)
2 cups canola oil
1 sweet potato, peeled and
    cut into 8 thin slices
Batter (see here)
1 Tbsp salt
4 bao, halved like burger buns
    (see note)
Sauce (see here)
4 sprigs cilantro, torn

The Message Bao can be found in the frozen-food aisle of most Asian grocery stores.

MC LYTE BAO (PAGE 40)

BULGOGI BEEF TOSTADAS

While bold Korean and Mexican flavours seem like an unlikely pairing, they work incredibly well together. Here, the sweet, stir-fried Korean beef, known as bulgogi, is offset by the freshness of Mexican toppings. Add the crunchy saltiness of the tostada and you've got yourself a perfect bite of food.

Bulgogi beef Combine all ingredients except beef in a bowl. Add beef to the marinade, stirring to coat. Cover and refrigerate for at least 8 hours.

Tomato-corn salsa Combine all ingredients in a bowl. Refrigerate until needed.

Lime crema Combine all ingredients in a bowl. Refrigerate until needed.

Makes 8

Prep 20 min, plus 8 hr marinating time
Cook 15 min

Bulgogi beef
3–4 slices ginger
1 clove garlic, coarsely chopped
½ pear, unpeeled, cut into sixths, and deseeded
1 Tbsp canola oil
½ tsp brown sugar
½ tsp sesame seeds
½ tsp soy sauce or tamari
9 oz *Certified Angus Beef* flank, thinly sliced on a bias

Tomato-corn salsa
1 Roma tomato, seeded and finely chopped
2 sprigs cilantro, finely chopped
½ jalapeño, seeded and finely chopped
⅓ cup corn kernels
¼ small red onion, finely chopped
1 tsp canola oil
Salt and black pepper to taste

Lime crema
¼ cup sour cream
Juice of ½ lime
Salt and black pepper to taste

Assembly Heat 2½ cups oil in a deep wok or frying pan over high heat to a temperature of 400°F. Add tortillas, two at a time, and deep-fry for 2–3 minutes, until crisp and golden brown. Using metal tongs, transfer to a plate lined with paper towel to drain. Season with salt. Repeat with the remaining tortillas. Keep warm.

Heat 2 tablespoons of the same oil in a frying pan over medium-high heat. Gently lower bulgogi beef into oil and cook for 1 minute. Turn over and cook for another minute, until beef is cooked to medium. Using a metal slotted spoon, transfer to a plate lined with paper towel to drain.

Place lettuce on each fried tortilla, then add 2 slices of avocado. Top with kimchi, bulgogi beef, and tomato-corn salsa. Using a squeeze bottle, drizzle with lime crema and garnish with spring onions, cotija, sesame seeds, and cilantro.

Serve immediately with lime wedges and radishes.

The Message Fry oil can be reused several times. Allow the oil to cool, then run it through a strainer to remove all impurities that might be left in it.

Make It Gluten-Free This dish can be made gluten-free by using tamari instead of soy sauce.

Assembly
2½ cups canola oil
8 (4-inch) corn tortillas
Salt to taste
Bulgogi Beef (see here)
1 cup chopped iceberg lettuce
1 ripe avocado, pitted and
   thinly sliced (16 slices)
½ cup finely chopped kimchi
Tomato-Corn Salsa (see here)
Lime Crema (see here)
1 spring onion, finely chopped
2 Tbsp crumbled cotija cheese
1 Tbsp toasted black
   sesame seeds
2 sprigs cilantro, hand torn
Lime wedges, to serve
Radishes, sliced, to serve
   (optional)

BULGOGI BEEF TOSTADAS (PAGE 44)

CHOP SUEY AND GRILLED CHEESE: TALES FROM THE WOK AND FLAT TOP

My first serious introduction to food was at my father's restaurant. Weekly trips were made with my grandparents to Chinatown to stock up on supplies for the kitchen. My grandfather would be behind the wheel of his baby blue Pontiac LeMans, often dangling a lit cigarette out the window, while my grandmother sat in the backseat and did her makeup, surrounded by bags of produce, meat, and fish. Part surrogate daycare, part kiddie cooking school, Highbell piqued my curiosity for how food was prepared. It was in this kitchen that I learned to garnish sweet-and-sour chicken balls, flip burgers, and roll jumbo eggrolls. I'd spend hours there each day after school, watching my grandparents cook up crowd-pleasing dishes that were, curiously... North American.

A consummate new-world Chinese eatery, the restaurant brought Hong Kong flavours to dishes that its Toronto patrons could get down with (cue those glorious chicken balls, banquet burgers, and jumbo eggrolls). Call 'em the gateway flavours to the development of an international palate—these classics ensured that the loyal customers who ordered our burger would soon take on the chop suey. (I'd often catch my classmates there, eating french fries during lunch break, and only much later in life did I understand that they were formulating the building blocks for their lifelong Chinese food addiction.) And hell yes, I dug those fries, too.

Those very dishes that many North Americans grew to love were the tasty foundation for my food journey, from my first grilled cheese creation with Kraft singles, gochujang, and kimchi (page 97) to a mean egg drop soup (page 74). In fact, some of those dishes still resonate with me today, the most popular ones reinvented with my signature spin. Some are featured in menus, while others are frequently prepared at home by me and my family.

素食

VEGE-
TARIAN

AVOCADO BOATS

This simple dish takes fresh, creamy avocado to the next level with a few easy steps and ingredients. Created for my growing plant-based eating clientele, it got enough positive feedback for me to confidently showcase it on *Cityline*.

Pico de gallo Combine all ingredients in a bowl.

Miso vinaigrette Combine all ingredients in a bowl, mixing until miso paste is dissolved.

Assembly Scoop a generous teaspoon of pico de gallo into the core of each avocado half. Drizzle avocado with vinaigrette, then garnish with furikake and parsley (if using). Serve immediately.

Make It Gluten-Free This dish can be made gluten-free by omitting the miso.

Serves 4

DF, QUICK, VEG
Prep 15 min

Pico de gallo
1 small vine-ripened tomato, finely chopped and drained
1 small clove garlic, finely chopped
⅓ jalapeño, seeded, deveined, and chopped (optional)
1 Tbsp finely chopped red onion
1 Tbsp finely chopped cilantro
1 tsp canola oil
Juice of ½ lime
Salt and black pepper to taste

Miso vinaigrette
1 tsp lemon juice
1 tsp rice vinegar
½ tsp canola oil
¼ tsp miso paste
¼ tsp agave nectar

Assembly
Pico de Gallo (see here)
2 large ripe avocados, halved and pitted
Miso Vinaigrette (see here)
¼ tsp vegan furikake
Finely chopped Italian parsley (optional)

GREEN BEAN BABY

Green beans get a bad rap. They are often underwhelming and uninspired, either bland or overcooked (or both). However, in many Chinese homes, green bean dishes, when cooked properly and paired with umami-loaded seasonings or sauces, explode with flavour. This popular Taiwanese-inspired version was served at Kanpai Snack Bar.

Bring a medium saucepan of water to a boil. Add beans and cooked for 4–5 minutes, until al dente and bright green. Drain, then rinse under cold running water.

Heat canola oil in a wok or frying pan over high heat. Add garlic and sauté for 1 minute, until fragrant. Add chili paste, chili oil, sugar, and soy sauce (or tamari) and stir to mix well. Add green beans and stir-fry for 1–2 minutes, until beans are coated and warmed through. If pan is dry, add 1–2 tablespoons water. Transfer to a serving platter.

Make It Gluten-Free This dish can be made gluten-free by using tamari instead of soy sauce.

Serves 2

DF, QUICK, VEG
Prep 5 min
Cook 5–10 min

5½ oz green beans, trimmed
1 Tbsp canola oil
1 clove garlic, finely chopped
1 Tbsp chili paste
1 tsp chili oil
1½ tsp sugar
1 tsp soy sauce or tamari

MEXICAN STREET CORN (*ESQUITES*)

Full of texture, flavour, and colours, this easy and tasty side dish works well with most meals, but especially tacos. Here it's kicked up a notch with a hit of Japanese seasoning.

Heat oil in a small saucepan over medium heat. Add corn and sauté for 2–3 minutes. Add lime juice and sauté for 3–5 minutes, until corn is heated through. Stir in sour cream, salt, and pepper.

Transfer mixture to a serving platter. Sprinkle with togarashi and garnish with queso fresco and cilantro. Serve with lime wedges.

Serves 2–4

GF, QUICK, VEG
Prep 10 min
Cook 10 min

2 Tbsp canola oil
2 cups corn kernels
Juice of 1 lime
½ cup sour cream
¼ tsp salt
¼ tsp black pepper
¼ tsp togarashi
¼ cup crumbled queso fresco
2 sprigs cilantro, chopped
Lime wedges, to serve

STEWED TOMATOES WITH EGGS (*FAN KEH LO DAN*)

This dish—often prepared by my mom for a midweek meal—speaks to some of my fondest childhood memories at the dinner table. And so many things make it right: it's quick and easy, and the sweet, tangy sauce brings the entire dish together.

Cut tomatoes in quarters, then halve each quarter.

Heat oil in a frying pan over high heat. Add eggs and scramble for 2–3 minutes, until just cooked through. Transfer to a plate.

Put tomatoes and ½ cup water in the same pan and simmer over medium heat for 3–4 minutes, until stewed. Add ketchup, salt, sugar, and pepper and mix well. Cover and simmer for another minute. Stir in spring onions and eggs.

In a small bowl, combine cornstarch with ½ teaspoon water and slowly add to the pan. Cook mixture for another minute, until thickened to a loose sauce. Turn off heat, cover, and let rest for a minute.

Transfer to a serving platter and garnish with cilantro. Serve with rice.

Serves 4

DF, GF, QUICK, VEG
Prep 10 min
Cook 10 min

4 hot house or vine-ripened
    tomatoes
2 tsp canola oil
2 eggs, beaten
2 tsp tomato ketchup
    (the secret!)
½ tsp salt
½ tsp sugar
⅓ tsp black pepper
2 spring onions, chopped
½ tsp cornstarch
Sprig of cilantro, hand torn,
    for garnish
Steamed rice, to serve

VEGETARIAN PROTEIN SOURCES

During my early involvement with the plant-based Fat Rabbit restaurant, I created a menu inspired by a combination of healthy and soulful flavours. A common concern about a vegetarian diet is its potential lack of protein, so when preparing vegetarian dishes, we look to a variety of protein sources. Here are some of my favourites.

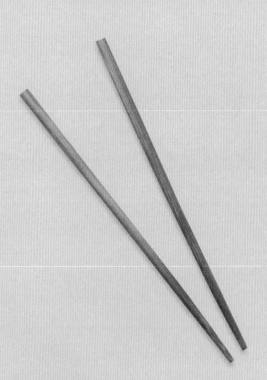

Almonds
6 g protein per 28 g

Beans (chickpeas, black beans, kidney, etc.)
16 g protein per 1 cup (cooked)

Chia seeds
6 g protein per 1 cup

Coconut
3 g protein per 1 cup

Edamame
11 g protein per 100 g

Eggs
6 g protein per large egg

Greek yogurt
23 g protein per 1 cup

Green peas
9 g protein per 1 cup

Hempseed
10 g protein per 28 g

Lentils
18 g protein per 1 cup (cooked)

Nutritional yeast
14 g protein per 28 g

Oats
12 g protein per 1 cup

Peanut butter
5-7 g protein per 28 g

Quinoa
8-9 g protein per 1 cup (cooked)

Seitan
25 g protein per 100 g

Soy milk
7 g protein per 1 cup

Spelt
10-11 g protein per 1 cup (cooked)

Sweet potato
3 g protein per 1 cup (cooked)

KUNG PAO-STYLE CAULIFLOWER WINGS

Adapting a classic North American Chinese dish to create a gluten-free, vegetarian version turned out to be a greatest hit. This quick, fuss-free recipe has been adapted for home cooks to prepare with ease. The kung pao sauce is a crazy flavour bomb, so don't hold back!

Kung pao sauce Pulse all ingredients in a food processor until smooth and emulsified. Transfer to a small saucepan and keep warm over low heat.

Cauliflower wings In a large bowl, combine cornstarch, garlic powder, cayenne, paprika, and salt. Add cauliflower and toss to coat. Transfer florets to a colander and shake off excess seasoning.

Heat oil in a deep fryer or a deep saucepan over high heat to 375°F. Using a metal slotted spoon, carefully lower cauliflower into the oil and deep-fry for 4–5 minutes, until florets are crisp and float to the surface. Transfer cauliflower to a plate lined with paper towel to drain.

Place cauliflower in a large bowl, add chili sauce, and toss to coat. Transfer to a serving platter and garnish with sesame seeds and spring onions.

Serves 4

DF, GF, QUICK, VEG
Prep 15 min
Cook 5 min

Kung pao sauce
¼ cup canola oil
¼ cup local honey or agave nectar
2½ Tbsp rice vinegar
2 Tbsp Sriracha
½ tsp chili flakes
1 clove garlic, finely chopped

Cauliflower wings
1 cup cornstarch
½ tsp garlic powder
½ tsp cayenne pepper
¼ tsp paprika
¼ tsp salt
1 head cauliflower, broken into 2-inch florets
Canola oil, for deep-frying
Sweet Chili Sauce (see here)
½ tsp toasted sesame seeds, for garnish
1 spring onion, sliced diagonally, for garnish

GUACAMAME

When I first opened La Brea, I wanted to offer a guacamole with an Asian spin. I had some shucked edamame in my fridge, so I pulsed them and then stirred the mix into my homemade guac. The added texture, familiar taste, and extra protein made for a fun and new way to enjoy a classic fave.

Using a large pestle and mortar, mash avocado and lime together. (Alternatively, use a food processor.) Stir in edamame, garlic, cilantro, and onions, then pound into a coarse mash. Add 2 tablespoons oil and the Sriracha (if using) and mix well. Season with salt and pepper, drizzle with more Sriracha (if using), then garnish with cilantro.

Heat the remaining 2½ cups oil in a deep fryer or a deep saucepan over high heat to 375°F. Using a metal slotted spoon, gently lower in a quarter of the tortillas and deep-fry for 3 minutes, until crisp and golden. Transfer to a plate lined with paper towel to drain. Repeat with the remaining tortillas and wonton wrappers. Season both with salt.

Transfer chips to a serving platter and serve with guacamame.

Make It Gluten-Free This dish can be made gluten-free by replacing the wontons with more corn tortillas.

Serves 2

DF, GF, QUICK, VEG
Prep 15 min
Cook 10–15 min

1 ripe avocado
Juice of 1 lime
1 cup shucked edamame
1 clove garlic, finely chopped
2 sprigs cilantro, finely chopped, plus extra for garnish
½ small onion, finely chopped
2½ cups + 2 Tbsp canola oil (divided)
Sriracha (optional)
Salt and black pepper to taste
8 (5-inch) corn tortillas, each cut into 6 equal wedges
8 large wonton wrappers, cut into 4 equal triangles

NOLA-STYLE VEGAN GUMBO

Gumbo is a dish I love but rarely make. As more diners opt for vegetarian and vegan alternatives, I wanted to push the envelope by introducing an inclusive, plant-based version of a recipe traditionally made with meat protein while still preserving the heart of the dish. This soulful gumbo is so full of goodness, so loaded with nutrient-rich veggies, and so packed with flavour, you won't miss the meat.

Preheat oven to 425°F.

Heat oil in a large saucepan over medium heat. Add onions and bell peppers and sauté for 5 minutes. Add garlic and cook for another minute, until fragrant. Stir in cayenne (or chili flakes) and cook for another minute.

Sear sausage in oven for 3–4 minutes on each side. Chop sausage into 1½-inch pieces.

Add sausage, tomatoes, and stock to the pan and bring to a boil over high heat. Stir in rice and parsley, reduce heat to medium-low, and simmer for 10 to 15 minutes, until vegetables are tender and sauce has slightly thickened. Season with salt and pepper. Garnish with cilantro.

Serves 4

DF, GF, VEG
Prep 10 min
Cook 30 min

1 Tbsp canola oil
1 large red onion, chopped
1 green bell pepper, seeded, deveined, and chopped
1 red or yellow bell pepper, seeded, deveined, and chopped
4 cloves garlic, finely chopped
1½ tsp cayenne pepper or chili flakes
4 plant-based sausages, defrosted
1 (28-oz) can diced tomatoes, undrained
1 cup vegetable stock
2 cups cooked brown rice
¼ cup chopped Italian parsley
Salt and black pepper to taste
Chopped cilantro, for garnish

LENTIL, EDAMAME, AND PEA SALAD

With the emergence of plant-based diets, creating dishes that go beyond leafy salads to fill your plate with bountiful protein and flavour is essential. Individually, these peas and legumes are quite delicious but combined they are even better. South Asian and Chinese ingredients provide spice and vegan sausage adds substance when mealtime calls for more than a simple salad.

Dressing Combine all ingredients in a bowl or mason jar.

Salad Heat oil in a frying pan over high heat. Add sausages (if using) and sear for 3 minutes on each side. Transfer to a plate.

Bring tikka masala to a simmer in a small saucepan. Add sausages and simmer for 15 minutes on low heat. Turn off heat and keep warm.

In a saucepan, bring lentils and 4 cups water to a boil. Boil for 12–15 minutes, until tender. Drain, then rinse under cold running water.

In a large bowl, combine corn, peas, edamame, tomatoes and herbs. Add lentils and toss gently to combine. Remove sausages from sauce and cut each into 4 segments.

Top salad with sausage and garnish with coconut and cashews (or almonds). Drizzle with dressing and season with salt and pepper. Serve immediately, topped with pea shoots (or micro daikon).

Serves 4

DF, GF, VEG
Prep 10 min
Cook 35 min

Dressing
2 Tbsp canola oil
2 Tbsp lemon juice
½ tsp chaat masala
½ tsp ground coriander
½ tsp cayenne pepper
Salt and black pepper to taste

Salad
1 Tbsp canola oil
2 plant-based sausages, defrosted (optional)
½ cup store-bought tikka masala sauce
½ cup red lentils
1 cup fresh or frozen corn kernels, defrosted if frozen
1 cup fresh or frozen peas, defrosted if frozen
1 cup shucked frozen edamame, defrosted if frozen
½ cup chopped heirloom cherry tomatoes
2 Tbsp chopped cilantro
2 Tbsp chopped Italian parsley
1 Tbsp unsweetened shredded coconut, for garnish
1 Tbsp halved cashews or almond slivers, for garnish
Small bunch of pea shoots or micro daikon, for garnish

RED QUINOA AND
SWEET POTATO HASH

I created this breakfast dish for a few hundred restaurant execs at a corporate meeting. I had been asked to highlight eggs, and I wanted to offer a healthy, balanced, forward-thinking dish. *Onsen tamago*, meaning "to cook slow in Japanese hot springs," can be mimicked with sous-vide.

With a sous-vide in a water bath, set water temperature to 147°F. Add whole eggs and cook for 47 minutes. Remove and let cool. When cracked open, whites should be milky and yolk should be whole but slightly runny inside. (Alternatively, a soft poach or a 7-minute soft-boiled egg works just as well.)

Rinse quinoa in a fine-mesh sieve under cold running water until water runs clear. Drain, then transfer to a medium saucepan. Add 2 cups water and salt and bring to a boil. Cover, reduce heat to medium-low, and simmer for 15–20 minutes, until all the liquid is absorbed. Let stand for 5 minutes, then fluff with a fork.

Heat oil in a frying pan over high heat. Add sweet potato and cook for 8–10 minutes, until slightly softened and caramelized. Add bell peppers, onions, and jalapeños and sauté for 2–3 minutes. Stir in tofu and sauté for another 2 minutes. Add stock, coriander, and togarashi, season with salt and pepper, and sauté for 5 minutes, until vegetables are cooked and stock has reduced to a third. Stir in quinoa, turn off heat, and cover. Let stand for 2–3 minutes.

Divide quinoa among 4 plates or shallow bowls. Carefully break open eggs, placing one on top of each serving of hash. Garnish with furikake. Serve immediately.

Serves 4

DF, GF, VEG
Prep 10 min
Cook 50 min

4 eggs
1 cup red quinoa
Salt and black pepper
   to taste
3 Tbsp canola oil
½ large sweet potato,
   peeled and finely chopped
1 red bell pepper, seeded,
   deveined, and finely chopped
½ red onion, finely chopped
1 jalapeño, seeded, deveined,
   and finely chopped
8 oz firm tofu, cut into
   ½-inch cubes
⅓ cup vegetable stock
1 Tbsp ground coriander
¼ tsp togarashi
1 Tbsp vegan furikake,
   for garnish

COCONUT CHIA PUDDING WITH MINTED PEACH

When my catering business Pop Kitchen began to flourish, I wanted to challenge convention by offering wholesome, healthier options at corporate events. The dishes we conceived were lighter and more balanced but still have flavour and depth. I love this recipe so much that I often have it in my fridge at home.

Combine chia seeds and coconut milk in a bowl and stir to submerge seeds. Cover and refrigerate the pudding for 2–3 hours.

Bring 1 cup water to a boil in a small saucepan. Add sugar and lemongrass. Reduce heat to medium-low and steep for 30–40 minutes. Strain.

Remove chia pudding from the refrigerator, mix in the chopped peaches and mint leaves, then sweeten to taste with lemongrass syrup.

Portion pudding into glasses and top with sliced peaches. Garnish with a mint leaf.

Serves 8

DF, GF, VEG
Prep 10 min, plus 2–3 hr soaking time
Cook 30–40 min

2/3 cup chia seeds
4 cups coconut milk
3 Tbsp sugar
1 stalk lemongrass, trimmed, peeled, and cut into thirds
1 ripe peach or nectarine, unpeeled, pitted, and finely chopped, plus extra sliced peaches for garnish
2–3 sprigs mint, leaves only, plus extra for garnish

SWEET EGG CUSTARD (*DUN DAN*)

Grandpa Ping, my mom's dad, was a poised and distinguished man who was seldom in the kitchen. But when he was, his patience and delicate manner shone through and magic would be created. To this day, I continue to strive for that level of perfection. This tasty dessert makes for a light treat at the end of a meal.

Combine sugar, finely chopped ginger, and 2 cups water in a small saucepan over medium heat. Simmer uncovered for 20 minutes, stirring occasionally, then set aside to cool. Strain syrup through a fine-mesh sieve.

Beat eggs in a bowl. Slowly whisk in syrup, then distribute the mixture evenly among 4 ramekins. Cover tightly with plastic wrap.

Bring water to a boil in a steamer. Place ramekins in steamer basket, cover, and steam for 20–25 minutes. Remove from heat and remove plastic film.

If desired, grate ginger over custard. Serve hot or at room temperature, garnished with thin strips of ginger.

Serves 4

DF, GF, VEG
Prep 10 min
Cook 40–45 min

2½ Tbsp brown sugar or rock sugar
2 slices ginger, finely chopped, plus extra for garnish
4 eggs

OG (AKA ORIGINAL GANGSTER) GENERATION: RECIPES OF OLD

We all have memories of dishes that have passed down through the generations, becoming integral parts of our family's story and the binding agents of big moments, from holiday dinners to birthday parties. This is a special kind of comfort food, which happily fills our bellies and lives on in our hearts and minds.

These culinary heirlooms rarely come with hand-written instructions. Instead, they are shared through sights, sounds, and tastes that act as sensory guide-posts through time. The first time Grandpa TK pulled that huge pan of baked pork chop rice out of the oven (page 150), I knew staff meal would be extra special that day. I cherish that memory to this day.

I've been blessed with a particularly acute sensory memory: my palate just *knows* its way back to Grandpa TK's kitchen. Intuition, for example, helped me identify the spice blend used in his famous Salted Fried Chicken Wings (page 84). (I'll let you in on a little secret: Grandpa's simple finishing spice is just fine salt and white pepper, heated in a pan over high heat to bring out the essence.) I have no recorded measurements or written instructions, just memories of watching my family prepare and assemble these dishes. The taste, the sound, the dashes, the pinches—I've recounted them in my own way for you here.

Like riding a bike, perfecting classics takes prac-tice. Over the past many years, I've managed to perfect the Lui family classics, from Mom's handmade wontons (page 29) to Grandpa Ping's Sweet Egg Custard (page 68), while adapting them for the North American palate. I've swapped many hard-to-get or outdated ingredients—for example, I use vegetable fat instead of pork lard (I also use canola oil instead of peanut oil), so that these recipes can be seamlessly recreated by any home cook.

While I can't tell you the number of times these dishes reappeared in our family's timeline, I can tell you how special they've been to us—and how to make 'em, too.

Baked Pork Chop over Rice
(*Guk Jui Pa Fan*) (page 150)

BBQ Pork on Rice (*Char Siu Fan*) (page 108)

Black Bean Spare Ribs
(*See Jup Pai Gwat*) (page 98)

Mapo Tofu (page 131)

Salted Fried Chicken Wings (*Ja Gai Yik*) (page 84)

Steamed Whole Fish (page 119)

Sweet Egg Custard (*Dun Dan*) (page 68)

XO Turnip Cake (*Lo Bok Go*) (page 34)

雞與雞蛋

CHICKEN & EGGS

BBQ PORK EGG FOO YOUNG

Known in our kitchen circle as a Chinese omelette, this delicious dish is as popular in North American Chinese restaurants as it is in Chinese households. (At home, it was more often called *chow dan*, which translates to "scrambled eggs.") It's best served as a family-style side with rice, vegetables, and protein.

Season eggs with a pinch of salt and pepper.

Heat oil in a non-stick frying pan over high heat. Add onions and BBQ pork and cook for 3–4 minutes, until onions are translucent. Slowly pour in egg mixture, then tilt pan to ensure the bottom is entirely covered. Season with salt and pepper and reduce heat to medium. Sprinkle spring onions over the egg mixture and, using a spatula to gently stir eggs, cook for 2 minutes, until edges are cooked. Flip eggs over and cook for another 2–3 minutes.

Garnish with cilantro or parsley and serve immediately with rice.

Serves 4 (family-style)

DF, GF, QUICK
Prep 5 min
Cook 10 min

4 eggs, beaten
Salt and black pepper to taste
1½ Tbsp canola oil
½ onion, finely chopped
5½ oz BBQ pork (*char siu*), chopped
1 spring onion, chopped
Chopped cilantro or Italian parsley, for garnish
Steamed rice, to serve

EGG DROP SOUP

Egg drop soup—a fortifying soup of ground meat, often pork, swirls of egg white, and fresh cilantro in a nourishing chicken stock—is especially comforting during the cold Canadian winter. I would often prepare stocks with vegetables and bones, then add whatever protein and vegetables were in the fridge. I like this lighter version made with ground turkey.

Heat canola oil in a medium saucepan over high heat. Add onions and carrots and sauté for 1–2 minutes, until slightly softened. Stir in sesame oil.

Add turkey and peas and sauté for 3 minutes. Stir in cilantro and ¼ teaspoon each salt and pepper. Add ½ cup water and mix, scraping the bottom of the pan, then bring the mixture to a boil.

Pour in stock and return soup to a boil, then reduce heat to low and simmer. Add eggs to the pan, stirring continuously to create strands of egg white. (The yolk colours and thickens the soup, leaving only the egg white strands visible.) Simmer for 10–12 minutes, then season with the remaining ¼ teaspoon each salt and pepper. Add cooked pasta (or rice) (if using).

Ladle soup into bowls and garnish with spring onions.

Make It Gluten-Free This dish can be made gluten-free by using rice instead of pasta.

Serves 4

DF, QUICK
Prep 10 min
Cook 20 min

1 Tbsp canola oil
¼ onion, finely chopped
½ small carrot, finely chopped
½ tsp sesame oil
1 cup cooked ground turkey
½ cup green peas
Sprig of cilantro, finely chopped
½ tsp salt (divided)
½ tsp white pepper (divided)
4 cups vegetable stock
2 eggs
2 cups cooked pasta of your
  choice or rice (optional)
1 spring onion, chopped,
  for garnish

MARBLE TEA EGGS

Teas eggs are important in Chinese culture, often served as snacks at home, in restaurants, and by street vendors. (In Taiwan, they are even available in major convenience stores.) My fondness for eggs coupled with pride for my heritage inspired this special tapas-style dish, with its uniquely modern twist.

Bring a medium saucepan of water to a boil. Gently lower in eggs and cook for 8 minutes. Using a slotted spoon, transfer eggs to a colander. Soak eggs in a cold water bath until they have completely cooled.

Using the back of a teaspoon, gently crack the entire surface of an egg. Do NOT peel. Repeat with the remaining eggs.

In a medium saucepan, bring soy sauce (or tamari) and 4 cups water to a boil. Reduce heat to medium-low and simmer. Add tea bags, cinnamon sticks, star anise, and sugar. Bring to a simmer, then reduce heat to low and steep mixture for 20–25 minutes. Turn off heat, add eggs, and let cool. Cover and let marinate in the refrigerator for at least 8 hours.

Drain eggs. Carefully remove shells. Spread pea shoots on a large plate, arrange the whole eggs on top, and garnish with flying fish caviar.

Make It Gluten-Free This dish can be made gluten-free by using tamari instead of soy sauce.

Makes 8

DF, VEG
Prep 10 min,
plus 8 hr marinating time
Cook 30–35 min

8 eggs
2 cups soy sauce or tamari
4 black tea bags
2 cinnamon sticks
1 star anise
2 tsp sugar
½ cup micro greens of choice (pea shoots or tatsoy is what I use), to serve
¼ cup orange or black flying fish caviar (tobiko), for garnish

EGG WHITE POLENTA STACK

All too often, breakfasts are carb-filled grease traps, so I constantly challenge our catering customers to choose dishes that fall outside that realm. This recipe is a lighter, healthier version of classic bacon and eggs.

Melt butter in a saucepan over medium-high heat. Add cornmeal and 1½ cups chicken stock and stir continuously until mixture reaches a simmer. Add another ¾ cup chicken stock and ½ cup water. Repeat again, then reduce heat to low and stir continuously until mixture has a thick porridge-like consistency. Turn off heat, cover, and let sit for 3 minutes.

Transfer polenta to a 9- × 13-inch baking pan or round mould. Spread evenly across the bottom, about ¾ inch deep. Set aside to cool, cover, and then refrigerate for at least 8 hours.

Cut polenta into 3-inch squares. (If you're using a round mould, cut into discs, 3 inches in diameter.)

Heat oil in a large frying pan over high heat. Add polenta pieces and reduce heat to medium-high. Pan-fry for 3 minutes, until seared and loosened from the pan. Turn over and cook for another 3 minutes. (Avoid poking or handling the polenta cakes too much or they will break.) If polenta begins to stick, add a little more oil or butter to the pan. Season with salt and pepper. Transfer to a plate.

In the same pan, fry bacon for 2–3 minutes on each side, until crisp. (It will cook more quickly than regular pork bacon.) Transfer to a plate lined with paper towel to drain and cool. Finely chop.

Heat pan with the residual bacon oil over high heat. Add egg whites and scramble for 2–3 minutes, until cooked through. Season with salt and pepper.

Place polenta cakes on plates and top with scrambled egg whites. Sprinkle with bacon bits and garnish with cilantro. Serve immediately with a dollop of crème fraîche (or salsa verde) (if using).

Serves 4

GF
Prep 15 min, plus 8 hr chilling time
Cook 20 min

1 Tbsp butter, plus extra if needed
1 cup coarsely ground cornmeal
3 cups chicken stock (divided)
3 Tbsp canola oil, plus extra if needed
Salt and black pepper to taste
5 slices turkey or chicken bacon
8 egg whites
Sprig of cilantro, finely chopped
Crème fraîche or salsa verde (optional)

MACANESE PORTUGUESE CHICKEN CURRY

I grew up on Hong Kong–style dishes, and exposed to the unique flavours of Macau (a former Portuguese colony), many of these dishes had a unique combination of European and Chinese flavours. This was one of our family favourites.

In a bowl, combine chicken, paprika, salt, and turmeric and mix with your hands. Set aside at room temperature while you prepare the other ingredients (or refrigerate for at least 8 hours).

Heat oil in a large saucepan over medium-high heat. Add onions and potatoes, reduce heat to medium-low, and sauté for 10 minutes. Add garlic and cook for another 5 minutes, until onions are cooked through and a glossy layer of oil rises to the surface. Add chicken and sauté for 4–5 minutes.

Pour in coconut milk, increase heat to medium-high, and bring to a near boil. Simmer mixture for 4 minutes, until slightly thickened, then reduce heat to medium-low and add fish sauce. Stir in 1½ cups water, increase heat to medium-high, and bring to a boil. (The stock will thin as the chicken starts to release its juices.)

Reduce heat to medium-low and simmer uncovered for 50 minutes, stirring occasionally, until the curry flavour has developed. (Droplets of paprika-red oil will rise to the surface; this is okay). Stir in curry powder and cayenne and simmer for another 15 minutes. Remove from heat and let stand for at least 20 minutes for the dish to develop more flavour as it cools. Season with more salt or fish sauce if needed. Drizzle chili oil overtop and garnish with cilantro. Serve with rice and wedges of lime (or lemon).

Serves 2

DF, GF
Prep 10 min, plus 8 hr marinating time, and 20 min standing time
Cook 1¼ hr

3 skinless, boneless chicken thighs, trimmed of excess fat and cut into bite-sized pieces
1 Tbsp paprika
2 tsp salt, plus extra to taste
½ tsp ground turmeric
⅓ cup canola oil
3 onions, finely chopped (3 cups)
1 large potato, peeled and cut into 1½-inch cubes
5 cloves garlic, finely chopped
1 (13½-oz) can coconut milk
1½ Tbsp fish sauce, plus extra to taste
1 tsp curry powder (such as Madras)
½ tsp cayenne pepper
1 Tbsp chili oil, for garnish
½ cup chopped cilantro, for garnish
Steamed rice, to serve
1 lime or lemon, cut into wedges, for garnish

TAIWANESE FRIED CHICKEN (AKA "THE ORIGINAL TFC")

This fried bird garnered acclaim, fame, and accolades in its lifetime, and not a week goes by without someone asking me about this infamous dish. We took an original Taiwanese flavour profile, added Western flair, and even made it gluten-free. Traditionally, at Taiwanese night markets, it is served as a boneless cutlet in a paper bag, but I've opted for southern style with side dishes and cold beer. My preferred pairing is an ice-cold Daura Damm for a completely gluten-free experience.

Rubbed chicken Rub chicken with salt and pepper, cover, and refrigerate for at least 2 hours but preferably up to 8 hours.

Batter Combine all the dry ingredients in a bowl. Add egg and 1 cup water and, using your hands, mix thoroughly. Add chicken and mix to thoroughly coat.

Assembly Heat oil in a deep fryer or deep saucepan over high heat to 375°F. Using a metal slotted spoon, carefully lower battered chicken pieces into the oil, submerging them. Deep-fry for 8–10 minutes, until the centre of the chicken has an internal temperature of 180°F. Transfer to a plate lined with paper towel to drain.

In a large bowl, combine chicken, white pepper, and salt and toss well. (For maximum flavour, first fry salt and pepper in a pan over high heat for 5–6 minutes, until fragrant.)

Transfer to a platter and garnish with chiles, spring onions, and cilantro. Serve with lemon wedges and sweet chili sauce (if using).

Serves 3–4

DF, GF
Prep 10 min, plus at least 2 hr resting time
Cook 20 min

Rubbed chicken
8–10 pieces chicken, drumsticks, thighs, and/or backs separated
½ tsp salt
½ tsp black pepper

Batter
½ cup cornstarch
½ cup tapioca starch
¾ cup custard powder (such as Bird's)
½ Tbsp salt
½ tsp black pepper
1 egg

Assembly
Vegetable oil, for deep-frying
½ tsp white pepper
½ tsp salt
4 bird's eye chiles, finely chopped
1 spring onion, finely chopped
6–8 sprigs cilantro, chopped
½ lemon, cut into wedges
Thai sweet chili sauce, to serve (optional)

SALTED FRIED CHICKEN WINGS (*JA GAI YIK*)

My Grandpa ᴛᴋ taught me to make this dish when I was eight years old. When I needed a quick fix, I could easily recreate it for myself. This version, served with a bright, spicy dipping sauce, is a nod to that classic.

Dipping sauce Combine all ingredients in a large bowl.

Chicken wings In a bowl, sprinkle wings with five-spice powder, ¼ teaspoon salt, and ¼ teaspoon black pepper, then turn wings to coat. Cover and refrigerate for 6 hours.

In a separate bowl, mix together flour, cornstarch, and 1 cup cold water until batter is smooth.

Heat oil in a deep fryer or deep saucepan over high heat to 375°F. Coat chicken with batter mixture. Using a metal slotted spoon, carefully lower chicken into the oil and deep-fry for 7–8 minutes, until wings are golden brown and crispy and the internal temperature is 180°F. Transfer to a plate lined with paper towel to drain.

In a clean bowl, combine chicken wings and the remaining ¼ teaspoon each salt and black pepper. Transfer to a plate and season with a pinch of salt and the white pepper. Serve immediately with the dipping sauce.

Serves 2–4 (as an appetizer)

DF
Prep 10 min,
plus 6 hr resting time
Cook 10 min

Dipping sauce
1 Tbsp light mayonnaise
1 tsp sambal oelek
½ tsp lime juice
1 spring onion, chopped
Salt and black pepper to taste

Chicken wings
6 whole chicken wings (drum, wing, and tip separated)
¼ tsp five-spice powder
½ tsp salt, plus extra to taste (divided)
½ tsp black pepper (divided)
½ cup all-purpose flour
¼ cup cornstarch
5 cups canola oil
½ tsp white pepper

MC HAMMER TAIWANESE POPCORN CHICKEN

Customers always asked about the name of this dish. When I was growing up in the eighties and nineties, MC Hammer was a popular music artist and, at one point, a branded celebrity for a fried chicken company. I recalled his Hammertime dance promoting popcorn chicken, and hence the name MC Hammer Taiwanese Popcorn Chicken. The dish, derived from Japanese karaage, makes for a great party snack or side dish.

In a medium mixing bowl, combine garlic, mirin, sesame oil, soy sauce (or tamari), and sugar. Add chicken to the marinade, stirring to coat. Cover and refrigerate for at least 8 hours.

Put potato starch in a medium bowl. Add chicken and stir well to ensure all pieces are thoroughly coated.

Heat oil in a medium saucepan over high heat. Using a metal slotted spoon, slowly lower chicken into the oil and deep-fry for 5–6 minutes, until golden, crispy brown and internal temperature is 180°F. Transfer chicken to a plate lined with paper towel to drain.

In a large bowl, combine chicken, salt, and pepper.

Using a metal slotted spoon, lower basil leaves into the hot oil and deep-fry for 6–8 seconds. Transfer leaves to a plate lined with paper towel to drain.

Garnish popcorn chicken with the basil leaves and serve immediately with chili (or plum) sauce.

Make It Gluten-Free This soup can be made gluten-free by using tamari instead of soy sauce.

Serves 2

DF
Prep 5 min, plus 8 hr marinating time
Cook 5–10 min

2 cloves garlic, finely chopped
2 tsp mirin
1 tsp sesame oil
1 Tbsp soy sauce or tamari
1 tsp sugar
2 skinless, boneless chicken thighs, cut into 1-inch pieces
1 cup potato starch
3 cups canola oil
½ tsp salt
½ tsp white pepper
8 Thai basil leaves
Chili sauce or plum sauce, to serve

CHICKEN OR THE EGG?

My relentless addiction to all things eggs includes this delicious sandwich, combining an award-winning fried chicken, farm-fresh eggs, and buttery brioche. I aspire to eat healthy most of the time, so long as I can balance it out with my guilty pleasure of fried chicken.

In a small bowl, sprinkle chicken with ¼ teaspoon salt, black pepper, and ¼ teaspoon white pepper, turning to coat well. Cover and refrigerate for at least 8 hours.

In a small bowl, combine custard powder, cornstarch, tapioca starch, and ½ cup water, mixing until smooth. Add 1 egg and mix well.

Heat 3 cups oil in a deep fryer or deep saucepan over high heat to 375°F. Dredge chicken pieces in batter, ensuring they are well and evenly coated. Using a metal slotted spoon, carefully lower chicken into the oil and deep-fry for 7 minutes, until the internal temperature of the chicken is 180°F. Transfer chicken to a plate lined with paper towel to drain. Season with the remaining ¼ teaspoon each salt and white pepper.

In a small bowl, mash avocado and stir in mayonnaise.

Heat a frying pan over high heat. Cook turkey bacon for 3 minutes on each side, until crisp. (Turkey bacon is generally precooked, so cooking time is fairly short.) Transfer to a plate lined with paper towel to drain.

Heat the remaining 2 tablespoons oil in the same pan over high heat. Add the remaining 4 eggs and cook for 2 minutes for sunny-side up.

Spread avocado mayonnaise onto the cut side of the top bun. (If you have extra, spread it on the bottom, too.) Place chicken, then 2 slices of bacon, on top. Carefully top with an egg and season with black pepper.

Serves 4

DF

Prep 10 min,
plus 8 hr resting time
Cook 20 min

2 skinless, boneless chicken
   thighs, halved lengthwise
½ tsp salt (divided)
½ tsp black pepper,
   plus extra to taste
½ tsp white pepper (divided)
½ cup custard powder
   (such as Bird's)
¼ cup cornstarch
¼ cup tapioca starch
5 eggs (preferably farm-fresh,
   divided)
3 cups + 2 Tbsp canola oil
   (divided)
1 small ripe avocado, pitted
2 Tbsp mayonnaise
8 slices turkey bacon
4 brioche buns or biscuits, halved

NASHVILLE HOT CHICKEN SANDWICH (PAGE 90)

NASHVILLE HOT CHICKEN SANDWICH

I was introduced to Nashville hot by a couple of young cooks, and I loved it so much that I enlisted those cooks as partners. We introduced Nashville's native bird at a pop-up concept to all the fine folks of Toronto. The level of heat spice depends on the amount of oil used to thin the finishing coat. We refer to it as the "slow burn" that keeps you coming back for more.

Marinated chicken In a bowl, combine buttermilk, pickle juice, salt, and cayenne. Add chicken, turning to thoroughly coat. Cover and refrigerate for at least 8 hours.

Slaw In a small bowl, combine all ingredients.

Nashville hot oil Heat oil in a small saucepan over medium-high heat to 300°F.

In a heatproof bowl, combine the remaining ingredients. Carefully pour in the hot oil, whisking continuously. Transfer mixture to the saucepan and keep over low heat, whisking occasionally.

Serves 4

Prep 20 min, plus 8 hr brining time
Cook 10 min

Marinated chicken
1 cup buttermilk
½ cup pickle juice
½ tsp salt
¼ tsp cayenne pepper
4 skinless, boneless chicken thighs

Slaw
¼ cup shredded green and purple cabbage
1 carrot, shredded
2 Tbsp apple cider vinegar
1 Tbsp canola oil
½ tsp sugar
¼ tsp salt

Nashville hot oil
1½ cups canola oil
2½ Tbsp cayenne pepper
½ Tbsp paprika
½ Tbsp garlic powder
1 tsp brown sugar
1–2 chiles of your choice (optional)

Batter In a medium bowl, whisk all ingredients together until smooth.

Dredge Combine flour and cornstarch in a medium bowl.

Assembly Heat oil in a deep fryer or deep saucepan over medium-high heat to 375°F. Place the batter and dredge by the pan of oil. One by one, submerge chicken thighs in the batter, then in the dredge to fully coat. Place on a wire rack. Using a metal slotted spoon, carefully lower chicken, one piece at a time, into the oil. (If necessary, work in batches to avoid overcrowding.) Deep-fry chicken for 7–8 minutes, until it has an internal temperature of 180°F. Transfer to a plate lined with paper towel to drain, then season with salt.

Whisk the Nashville hot oil to thoroughly mix ingredients again. Using tongs, carefully lower chicken into the oil to coat.

Smear butter on the cut side of brioche buns and toast. Place each bun on a plate.

Place a chicken thigh on each bottom bun. Garnish with slaw and a few slices of pickles. Top with the top bun and serve immediately.

Batter
⅔ cup all-purpose flour
2 Tbsp cornstarch
½ cup buttermilk
1 egg

Dredge
⅔ cup all-purpose flour
1 Tbsp cornstarch

Assembly
4 cups canola oil
Batter (see here)
Dredge (see here)
Marinated Chicken (see here)
⅓ tsp salt
Nashville Hot Oil (see here)
2 tsp butter
4 full-sized brioche buns, halved
Slaw (see here)
16 slices bread and butter pickles

THREE-NATIONS CHICKEN

Sometimes a dish comes together intentionally, other times, it's situational. In the case of this dish, I had forgotten certain ingredients for a cooking workshop, so I had to improvise. I assembled ingredients to prepare dishes with Korean, Taiwanese, and Japanese flavours, and this medley turned out to be a perfectly balanced mix—and the hit of the night.

Chili-honey sauce In a bowl, combine all ingredients.

Three-nations chicken In a large bowl, combine garlic, ginger, tamari, mirin, salt, and black pepper. Add chicken, stirring to coat. Cover and refrigerate for at least 8 hours.

Heat oil in a frying pan over high heat. Place potato starch in a shallow bowl and dredge marinated chicken. Place chicken in a colander and shake off excess starch. Add chicken to the pan and cook for 8 minutes, until golden brown and the internal temperature is 180°F. Using a metal slotted spoon, transfer chicken to a plate lined with paper towel to drain. Season with white pepper and salt.

Assembly In a large bowl, toss chicken with the chili-honey sauce, spring onions, cilantro, chiles, and sesame seeds, coating thoroughly. Transfer to a serving platter and serve with lemon wedges.

Serves 4 (as an appetizer)

DF, GF
Prep 15 min,
plus 8 hr marinating time
Cook 10 min

Chili-honey sauce
1½ Tbsp local honey or
   agave nectar
1 Tbsp gochujang paste
2 tsp tamari
1 tsp chili oil
1 clove garlic, finely chopped
Juice of ½ lime

Three-nations chicken
2 cloves garlic, finely chopped
2 Tbsp finely chopped ginger
3 Tbsp tamari
3 Tbsp mirin
2 tsp salt, plus extra to taste
1 tsp black pepper
4 skinless, boneless chicken
   thighs, cut into 1-inch pieces
¼ cup canola oil
1 cup potato starch
1 tsp white pepper,
   plus extra to taste

Assembly
Three-Nations Chicken (see here)
Chili-Honey Sauce (see here)
1 spring onion, sliced diagonally
½ bunch of cilantro,
   coarsely chopped
3–4 bird's eye chiles,
   finely chopped
½ tsp tuxedo sesame seed blend
1 lemon, cut into wedges

EASY LIKE SUNDAY MORNING

Our sense of smell is a wondrous thing. In an instant, the familiar scent of a dish can bring a flood of joyful memories. My nose often takes me back to Sunday mornings growing up, when there would be, without fail, an epic feast underway. Although my family ate quite a few meals together each week, Sunday's was the big one: my mom was always busy boiling up a bone broth that would act as a base to build flavour upon. It was a day off for everyone, and one completely anchored around the dining room table.

As I grew older, Sunday mornings invariably came with a hangover (sorry, Mom and Dad), and those dishes also doubled as my cure. For example, Sunday Congee (page 154) is highly recommended for mornings spent cursing yourself for that one last round of shots you ordered the night before.

I can still hear the laughs, the slurps, and the clanking of dishes at that Sunday table. I believe that the dining table is sacred, and it's lost on me how we have allowed some of the most important traditions to escape us. I no longer have Sunday morning meals like I did as a kid, but I do cherish family and friends gathering for a memorable meal, and the stories that creates. That, coupled with new dining experiences, has helped keep the tradition alive in my heart and inspires me to continue creating.

These family favourite recipes—plus a few new-to-the-roster recipes such as Ramen with L.A. Kalbi (page 164), which is my daughter's favourite—have seen me through my highest and lowest moments, and bring me back to that special time. Sundays.

温馨食品

COMFORT FOODS

GRILLED CHEESE REBOOTED

My tough-as-nails grandma ruled the fryer and griddle line of the kitchen. Here, she prepared mean burgers, fries, club sandos, and of course, grilled cheese sandwiches. I was taught this simple dish at a young age and, over the years, I experimented with whatever pantry ingredients I had on hand. Here's a version I still love to this day.

In a small bowl, combine ketchup and gochujang and set aside.

In a separate bowl, combine kimchi and pear.

In another bowl, combine butter and Sriracha. Using a small pastry brush, spread Sriracha butter on one side of each bread slice.

Heat a frying pan over medium-high heat. Place 2 slices of bread, butter side down, in the pan and reduce heat to medium. Sprinkle cheese over each slice. Add kimchi and pear. Add the 2 remaining bread slices, butter side up. Using a spatula, carefully flip over sandwiches, one at a time, and sear for 2–3 minutes, until slightly crispy. Turn off heat, cover pan, and cook sandwiches over residual heat for 1 minute, until cheese has melted.

Transfer to plates and cut in half diagonally. Serve with gochujang ketchup.

Makes 2 sandwiches

QUICK, VEG
Prep 10 min
Cook 5–10 min

3 Tbsp ketchup
1 Tbsp gochujang paste
½ cup kimchi, cut into thin strips
¼ Asian pear (or Bosc),
    cut into thin strips
¼ cup (½ stick) salted butter,
    melted
2 Tbsp Sriracha
4 slices whole grain and
    sprouted-seed bread
1 cup shredded 3-cheese blend

BLACK BEAN SPARE RIBS (*SEE JUP PAI GWAT*)

When I was growing up, everyone in my family would calculate where at the table they would sit in order to finagle their preferred cuts of spare ribs (I loved the pieces with a little bit of fat attached). We'd all also clamour for the sauce that remained on the serving platter. Near the end of the meal, I'd sometimes dump my rice onto the platter to soak up the savoury sauce, much to my mother's dismay. But how could I be faulted for valuing its goodness?

In a bowl, combine black bean sauce, garlic, soy sauce (or tamari), sugar, pepper, 2 teaspoons oil, and 1 teaspoon cold water. Add cornstarch, stirring until smooth. Add ribs to the marinade, turning to coat. Cover and refrigerate for 30 minutes.

Transfer ribs to a shallow plate and drizzle with the remaining 2 teaspoons oil.

Fill a steamer bottom (or large saucepan) halfway with water, cover, and bring to boil. Reduce heat to medium-high and place the plate in a steamer pot or bamboo steamer basket. Place over the hot water, cover, and cook for 10 minutes. Remove from heat.

Garnish with spring onions, cilantro, and chiles. Serve with rice.

Make It Gluten-Free This soup can be made gluten-free by using tamari instead of soy sauce.

Serves 4

DF
Prep 10 min, plus 30 min marinating time
Cook 10 min

1¼ Tbsp black bean sauce (such as Lee Kum Kee)
2 cloves garlic, finely chopped
1 Tbsp soy sauce or tamari
¾ tsp sugar
½ tsp black pepper
4 tsp canola oil (divided)
1 tsp cornstarch
1¼ lbs pork side ribs, cut into 1-inch-thick spare ribs (ask your butcher)
1 spring onion, sliced diagonally, for garnish
Sprig of cilantro, coarsely chopped, for garnish
1 bird's eye chile, finely chopped, for garnish
Steamed rice, to serve

CHINESE MEATLOAF WITH PRESERVED VEGETABLES (*JING YUK BANG*)

Often served at family-style dinners, this simple yet delectable meatloaf is unlike anything you've eaten. Ground pork is combined with shiitake mushrooms and preserved mustard greens and then steamed. In some households, prior to cooking, the mixture is scooped up by hand and then thrown back into the bowl, in order to make the pork adhere to itself better, reduce gaps between the pork fibres, and create more stickiness. But in our house, the greatest commotion was around who dug the spoon into the dish for the first bite.

Pour 1 cup hot water in a small bowl. Add mushrooms and soak for 1 hour. Remove mushrooms, reserving soaking liquid, then stem mushrooms and finely chop.

Place pork, mushrooms, and mustard greens in a large bowl and, using your hands, mix together. Add sugar, salt, and pepper.

In a wide, shallow, heatproof bowl, spread pork mixture to evenly cover the bottom; it should be ½ inch thick. Sprinkle 2½ tablespoons water evenly over the meat. (The water soaks up the flavours of the meat and seasoning and becomes the coveted sauce, or *jup*, that we fought over.) Cover with plastic wrap.

Fill a steamer (or a large saucepan) halfway with water, cover, and bring to boil. Reduce heat to medium-high and place the plate into a steamer pot or a bamboo steamer basket. Cover and cook for 10–12 minutes, until meat is firm and juicy. Remove from heat and carefully remove plastic wrap. Serve with rice.

Serves 4

DF, GF
Prep 10 min,
plus 1 hr soaking time
Cook 10–15 min

4 dried shiitake
   mushrooms, rinsed
14 oz ground pork
¼ cup preserved mustard greens,
   drained and finely chopped
¼ tsp sugar
¼ tsp salt
¼ tsp white pepper
Steamed rice, to serve

THE HIGHBELL BANQUET BURGER

A modern version of our classic banquet burger that Grandma used to make on the flat-top griddle. The burger was something she took to very quickly, considering that she had no formal culinary training or prior experience with Western food. The burger needs some fat content, so I use medium ground (as opposed to lean) ground beef; however, I've also combined it with turkey and chicken to create a more modern, healthier patty.

Patties In a bowl, combine all ingredients. Divide mixture in half and shape each portion into a 1-inch-thick patty. Cover and refrigerate for 1 hour.

Assembly Butter the cut side of the brioche buns.

Heat 2 tablespoons oil in a large frying pan over medium-high heat. Add mushrooms, reduce heat to low, and move to one side of the pan. Add mortadella to the other side and sear for 2–3 minutes on each side. Transfer mushrooms and mortadella to a plate.

Heat the remaining 2 tablespoons oil in the same pan over high heat. Add patties, reduce heat to medium-high, and cook 3–4 minutes, until they begin to caramelize and crust at the edges. Flip, then cook for another 3–4 minutes, until browned and caramelized at the edges. Add 3 tablespoons water to the pan, cover, and reduce heat to low. Cook for 2 minutes, until the internal temperature of the patties is 175°F. Cook for another 30 seconds. Place cheese on patties, then cover the pan and remove from heat.

In a separate pan, toast brioche for 1 minute on each side, until bun edges begin to brown. Spread dressing on the top half of each brioche bun.

Layer each bottom bun with lettuce and tomato followed by a patty, some mushrooms, and lastly, the mortadella. Top with a dressed bun top. Serve immediately.

Serves 2

Prep 10 min, plus 1 hr resting time
Cook 20 min

Patties

4 oz *Certified Angus Beef* medium ground chuck
4 oz ground turkey
4 oz ground chicken
1 shallot, finely chopped
1 small clove garlic, finely chopped
2 Tbsp breadcrumbs
½ tsp Worcestershire sauce
¼ tsp dried cilantro
¼ tsp salt
¼ tsp black pepper
1 egg

Assembly

2 tsp butter
2 brioche burger buns
4 Tbsp canola oil (divided)
6–8 cremini mushrooms, sliced
1¾ oz hot mortadella (such as San Daniele's) (2 thick slices)
Patties (see here)
Slices of semi-soft cheese, such as Taleggio
2 Tbsp Russian dressing
2 large green lettuce leaves
1 Roma tomato, thinly sliced

THE LAST SAMURAI

It's been a lifelong dream of mine to set up a food establishment in a space I've been frequenting since I was a child: the iconic Food Building at the Canadian National Exhibition, the oldest and largest fair of its kind in Canada. A trip to the fair meant a journey of planned eats. Since tasting my first ramen burger in New York, courtesy of chef Keizo Shimamoto, I've wanted a shot at recreating one of these scrumptious burgers, which combines a culinary trinity of my favourite things: ramen, burgers, and fried chicken.

Slaw Combine all ingredients in a bowl. Cover and refrigerate for at least 8 hours.

Rubbed chicken Rub chicken with salt and pepper. Cover and refrigerate for at least 2 hours but preferably at least 8 hours.

Patties Combine all ingredients in a bowl. Shape mixture into 4 patties, each about 1 inch thick. Cover and refrigerate for 1 hour.

Ramen buns Cook ramen (or noodles) according to package directions until al dente. Rinse under cold running water and drain thoroughly. In a bowl, combine ramen and eggs and mix thoroughly.

Heat a non-stick frying pan over medium-high heat. Divide ramen mixture into 8 equal portions. Place a 4-inch ring mould in the pan and fill it with a portion of ramen mixture; it should be about ¾ inch high. Cook for 3–4 minutes, until crispy and golden on the bottom. With a spatula, carefully flip the mould with the ramen in place and press down. Cook for another 3–4 minutes, until crisp. Transfer to a plate lined with paper towel to drain. Repeat with the remaining ramen.

Serves 4

Prep 25 min,
plus 8 hr resting time
Cook 35 min

Slaw
1½ cups shredded purple
   cabbage
1 Tbsp apple cider vinegar
1 tsp canola oil
½ tsp salt
½ tsp sugar
Black pepper to taste

Rubbed chicken
2 skinless, boneless chicken
   thighs, halved crosswise
Salt and black pepper to taste

Patties
14 oz ground chuck
1 shallot, finely chopped
1 small clove garlic, finely
   chopped
1 egg
2 Tbsp breadcrumbs
½ tsp Worcestershire sauce
¼ tsp dried cilantro
¼ tsp salt
¼ tsp black pepper

Ramen buns
2 (13-oz) packs ramen or
   chow mein egg noodles
2 eggs, beaten
2 Tbsp canola oil

Spicy aioli Combine all ingredients in a small bowl.

Fried chicken Combine custard powder, cornstarch, tapioca starch, 1 teaspoon salt, and black pepper in a bowl. Add egg and ½ cup water and, using your hands, mix thoroughly. Add chicken, stirring to coat well.

Heat oil in a deep fryer or deep saucepan over medium-high heat to 375°F. Using a metal slotted spoon, carefully lower chicken pieces into the oil, submerging them. Deep-fry for 8–10 minutes, until the centre of the chicken has an internal temperature of 180°F. Transfer to a plate lined with paper towel to drain.

In a large bowl, combine chicken, the remaining ½ teaspoon salt, and white pepper.

Assembly Heat oil in a frying pan over high heat. Add patties and reduce heat to medium-high. Cook for 3–4 minutes, until patties begin to crust around the edges. Flip patties and cook for another 3–4 minutes. Add 1–2 tablespoons water, cover, and reduce heat to medium-low. Cook for another 2 minutes, until the internal tempera-ture reaches 175°F. Place cheese on top of patties, cover, and cook for 1–2 minutes, until cheese has melted.

Place ramen buns on a plate. Place a burger patty on each, and then a fried chicken cutlet on top. Add slaw and a drizzle of aioli. Top sand-wiches with bun tops. Now eat.

Spicy aioli
½ cup Kewpie mayonnaise
1 tsp Sriracha
½ tsp chili oil

Fried chicken
½ cup custard powder
  (such as Bird's)
¼ cup cornstarch
¼ cup tapioca starch
½ Tbsp salt (divided)
½ Tbsp black pepper
1 egg
Rubbed chicken (see here)
Vegetable oil, for deep-frying
½ tsp white pepper, plus
  extra to taste

Assembly
2 Tbsp canola oil
Patties (see here)
4 slices American cheddar
Ramen Buns (see here)
Fried Chicken (see here)
Slaw (see here)
Spicy Aioli (see here)

THE LAST SAMURAI (PAGE 102)

PORK BONE SOUP

Family soups, particularly herbal renditions, are an essential part of any traditional Chinese meal, because it's believed that a soup symbolically opens up our heart and soul, detoxifies and nourishes the body, and staves off diseases. To be honest, I'm not a massive herbal soup fan, but I love this one. Look for precut meaty pork neck bones, which are full of flavour and, along with the lotus roots and yams, pair beautifully with soy sauce once removed from the soup. The pork stock is also a great base for soup noodles.

Place pork bones in a stockpot, cover with water, and bring to a boil over high heat. Boil for 2 minutes, then remove from heat and drain. Rinse bones thoroughly under cold running water to rinse off any impurities.

Bring 5½ quarts water to a boil in the same stockpot. Add pork bones and the remaining ingredients except salt and pepper and return to a boil. Reduce heat to medium-low and simmer uncovered for 4 hours, stirring occasionally, until fully rich in flavour. Season with salt and pepper.

Remove pot from heat and strain stock, reserving meat and herbs. Return stock to the pot and simmer, skimming off any residual fat from the surface.

Serve soup as a starter with the bone mixture on the side, along with a small dish of soy sauce (or tamari) for dipping.

The Message The ingredients used in this soup may be new to many home cooks, but they are essential to most homemade Chinese herbal soups. The dried items used to be found only in specialty shops; now they are readily available in the dried herbal ingredient aisles of Asian grocery stores.

Make It Gluten-Free This soup can be made gluten-free by using tamari instead of soy sauce.

Serves 4

DF
Prep 5 min
Cook 4 hr

2 lbs meaty pork neck bones
3 dried honey dates (see note)
3½ oz lotus root (see note)
4½ Tbsp pearl barley
3 Tbsp dried Chinese yam
  (see note)
2½ Tbsp dried lotus seeds
  (see note)
1 Tbsp goji berries
Salt and black pepper to taste
Soy sauce or tamari, to serve

BBQ PORK ON RICE (CHAR SIU FAN)

Great with steamed rice, noodles, bao (Chinese buns), toasted sandwiches, or on its own, Chinese-style BBQ pork is a Chinese household staple. I prefer a cut of pork shoulder or butt with a slight layer of fat cap (in Cantonese, we call this *boon fay sow*, which translates to "half fat-lean"), for maximum flavour.

Trim pork into 4 equal pieces.

In a large bowl, combine all ingredients except pork and honey. Reserve 2 tablespoons of the marinade in a small bowl, refrigerating until needed.

Add pork to the remaining marinade, using your hands to turn and fully coat the pork. Set on a plate, cover, and refrigerate for at least 10 hours.

Preheat oven to 400°F. Line a roasting pan with aluminum foil, ensuring all corners are covered and there are no holes. Pour 1 cup water into the pan, place a wire rack overtop (the rack should rest just above the water), and add the pork pieces, spreading them out. Roast for 15 minutes, until the fat and juices have accumulated in the pan. Add 1–2 tablespoons of the drippings to the reserved marinade. Turn over pork and cook for another 15 minutes.

Meanwhile, in a small saucepan, mix together the marinade mixture, 1 tablespoon water, and honey and heat over low heat until warm.

Once pork has an internal temperature of 160°F and is firm to the touch, remove from the oven. Using a pastry brush, baste one side of the pork with the marinade. Increase oven setting to broil, then broil pork, basted side up, for 5–7 minutes, until slightly caramelized and crisp. Turn over pork, baste, and broil for another 5–7 minutes. Remove from oven, loosely cover with foil, and let rest for 10 minutes.

Transfer the remaining pan drippings to a saucepan and simmer for 3–5 minutes, until slightly reduced. Slice pork and serve over rice, drizzled with sauce.

Serves 4

DF
Prep 10 min, plus 10 hr marinating time
Cook 40 min

2¼ lbs pork shoulder/ pork butt, fat on
¼ cup brown sugar
2 cloves garlic, finely chopped
1 Tbsp soy sauce or tamari
1 Tbsp canola oil
1 tsp Chinese cooking wine (Shaoxing)
1 tsp hoisin sauce
1 tsp molasses
¼ tsp five-spice powder
⅛ tsp white pepper
⅛ tsp black pepper
1 Tbsp local honey
Steamed rice, to serve

Make It Gluten-Free
This dish can be made gluten-free by using tamari instead of soy sauce.

STEPHANIE'S MOOSHIE MOOSHIE

This was my sister Stephanie's favourite dish when she was young. The name refers to the way she, as a toddler, described the cooked vegetables—as mushy. Since then, the dish has been known as "mooshie mooshie." It continues to have pride of place on the menu, as my sister now prepares it for her kids, using the same fun moniker. Ask your butcher to cut up the spare ribs (or look for them at your local Asian grocery stores and ask the butcher there to cut them).

In a large bowl, combine half the garlic, wine, soy sauce, cornstarch, and 2 tablespoons water. Add ribs to the marinade, turning to coat well. Cover and refrigerate for 45–60 minutes.

Heat 1 tablespoon oil in a large frying pan over high heat. Add ribs, reduce heat to medium-high, and sear for 4 minutes on each side, until browned. Transfer to a plate lined with paper towel to drain.

Heat the remaining 1 tablespoon oil in the same pan over medium-high heat. Add onions and the remaining garlic and sauté for 2–3 minutes, until onions are translucent. Stir in potatoes and cook for another 2 minutes. Add tomatoes and cook for 1 minute.

Add 3 cups water and bring to a simmer. Stir in oyster sauce and hoisin sauce, then the ribs. Reduce heat to medium-low, cover, and simmer for 25 minutes, until potatoes are cooked through. Add more water if needed so that the pan doesn't get too dry. Using the back of a fork, lightly mash potatoes until they are "mooshie" (you may need to add a bit more water). If sauce is thin, thicken with 1 tablespoon cornstarch slurry.

Transfer to a serving platter and serve with rice.

Serves 4

DF
Prep 10 min, plus 45–60 min marinating time
Cook 40 min

2 cloves garlic, finely chopped (divided)

2 tsp Chinese cooking wine (Shaoxing)

1 Tbsp sweet soy sauce (kecap manis)

1 Tbsp cornstarch, plus extra if needed

1 rack pork side ribs, cut into 1¼-inch pieces (ask your butcher)

2 Tbsp canola oil (divided)

1 sweet onion, finely chopped

4 russet potatoes, cut into ¼-inch cubes

1 vine-ripened tomato, finely chopped

2 Tbsp oyster sauce

1 Tbsp hoisin sauce

Steamed rice, to serve

BACK IN TIME: DONNING THE APRON AGAIN

Some recipes and dishes have helped me regain the bright-eyed wonder I had as a kid, back at my family's restaurant. Not to get too dramatic, but let's call it my rebirth.

After I graduated from university, I became fixated on landing the perfect job, earning the perfect salary, and making a perfect life . . . you know, all the goals that my well-intentioned parents set for me to achieve. But after two decades of climbing the corporate ladder, I'd lost my creative edge and soul. I wanted to be back in the kitchen. Hell, maybe even own my own restaurant one day!

It was around that time that I got my first taste of food-truck culture, in Los Angeles. I chased Roy Choi's Kogi food truck in hopes of biting into that kalbi taco, because his story—particularly his upbringing, his food, and the themes of his establishments—resonated with me. His food and identity are celebrated in every facet of the dining experiences he creates, and have inspired me to do this as well. When I returned home to Toronto, I threw on an apron and experimented every night after work.

My first pop-up, La Brea, named after the famed L.A. street, was a Mexican-Asian (I dubbed it "Mexic-Asian") mash-up. The menu was based on classic Mexican items such as sopas (page 25), queso, and tacos, but it included Asian ingredients such as barbequed pork and bulgogi (Korean grilled beef). We made wonton tacos, edamame guacamole aka Guacamame (page 58), and Asian-inspired

empanadas. That rush of working a service line and chatting with people who were enjoying my food had me hooked. Here are just some of the recipes from that fortuitous first outing.

Black Bean Chicken Taco (page 33)

Bulgogi Beef Tostadas (page 44)

Chips with the Dip: The Larry O.B. (page 27)

Corn and Chorizo Sopas (page 25)

Guacamame (page 58)

Mexican Street Corn (*Esquites*) (page 53)

家常菜

FAMILY STYLE

PRAWN RENDANG

I remember the first time I made traditional beef rendang. It was family holiday dinner and I wanted to do something with my new love for Indonesian cuisine. The family loved it! So much so that I've adapted the recipe many times and this seafood version is a personal favourite.

Pulse garlic, onion, chiles, ginger, lemongrass, turmeric powder, and oil in a food processor until smooth. Transfer to a frying pan over medium-high heat and bring to a simmer.

Add coconut milk, coconut, kaffir and turmeric leaves and simmer for 4–5 minutes. Add salt and sugar and allow to cook for 2–3 minutes until fully dissolved. Add bell pepper, and mix.

Add prawns and gently stir for 2–3 minutes. Lower heat to low and allow prawns and sauce to cook and reduce for an additional 2 minutes.

Transfer to a plate and garnish with cilantro and micro greens. Serve with roti canai.

Make It Gluten-Free This recipe can be made gluten-free by serving rice instead of roti canai.

Serves 2–4

DF, QUICK
Prep 15 min
Cook 12 min

4 cloves garlic
½ medium red onion
4 bird's eye chiles (or dried chiles)
1 Tbsp fresh ginger root, peeled
1 stalk lemongrass
1 tsp turmeric powder
¼ cup canola oil
¾ cup coconut milk
2 Tbsp shredded coconut
1 kaffir lime leaf
1 turmeric leaf
2 tsp salt
1½ tsp brown sugar
⅓ red bell pepper, seeded, deveined, and diced
12 large prawns, shelled with tails intact and deveined
Cilantro, finely chopped, for garnish
Micro greens of choice, for garnish
Fresh roti canai or steamed rice, to serve

CHICKEN CHOP SUEY (*GAI JAUP WUY*)

Jaup wuy in Cantonese loosely translates as "mixed up." In many households, it was a way to make a stir-fry with the mélange of leftover vegetables in the fridge. In North American Chinese restaurants, however, it evolved into a dish based on bean sprouts. This version is given a healthy, modern-day spin with the addition of superfood kale.

Heat 2 tablespoons oil in a wok or a large frying pan over medium-high heat. Add garlic and cook for 30 seconds, until fragrant. Add chicken and season with salt and pepper. Stir-fry for 7–8 minutes, until evenly cooked. Transfer chicken to a plate lined with paper towel to drain.

Heat the remaining 1 tablespoon oil in the same pan over medium-high heat. Add celery and carrots and sauté for 1–2 minutes. Add bean sprouts and sauté for another minute. Add mushrooms and kale.

Stir in soy sauce (or tamari), sugar, and ¼ cup water. Season with salt and pepper and sauté for 1½ minutes. Add chicken and stir-fry for another minute.

In a small bowl, combine cornstarch with 1½ tablespoons water. Stir 1 teaspoon of the mixture at a time into the sauce, simmering until the sauce is thick enough to coat the back of a wooden spoon.

Transfer to a serving platter. Garnish with cilantro and serve with rice.

The Message Chinese celery, a skinnier version of regular celery, has thin, hollow, crunchy stalks and a strong flavour. It can be found at most Asian grocery stores.

Make It Gluten-Free This dish can be made gluten-free by using tamari instead of soy sauce.

Serves 2-4

DF, QUICK
Prep 10 min
Cook 15 min

3 Tbsp canola oil (divided)
1 clove garlic, finely chopped
1 skinless, boneless chicken breast, sliced
Salt and black pepper to taste
4 stalks Chinese celery with tops, cut into thin strips (see note)
1 carrot, cut into thin strips
3 cups bean sprouts
8 shiitake mushrooms, sliced
1 cup loose chopped kale
1 Tbsp soy sauce or tamari
¼ tsp sugar
1 tsp cornstarch
2 sprigs of cilantro, hand torn, for garnish
Steamed rice, to serve

SESAME GINGER CHICKEN

This is a simple way to elevate chicken (or any protein, for that matter) as a quick, delicious meal. At home, this would be a protein dish alongside two to three other dishes—fish, vegetables, and rice or noodles—for a family-style meal.

Heat oil in a frying pan over high heat. Add chicken to the pan, season with salt and pepper, and sauté for 2–3 minutes, until chicken is cooked on the outside. Transfer to a plate lined with paper towel, to drain.

In the same pan over high heat, combine garlic, sugar, ginger, tamari, citrus juice, and hoisin and bring to a simmer. Cook for 3 minutes. Stir in chicken and simmer for another 4–5 minutes, until chicken is fully cooked.

In a small bowl, mix cornstarch and 1 tablespoon cold water. Add mixture to the pan, a little at a time, to thicken as desired. Transfer chicken to a plate, then garnish with sesame seeds and spring onions.

Serves 2–4

DF, GF, QUICK
Prep 10 min
Cook 15 min

2 Tbsp canola oil
1½ skinless, boneless chicken breasts, cut into ¼-thick strips
Salt and black pepper to taste
1 clove garlic, finely chopped
2 Tbsp brown sugar
1 tsp finely chopped ginger
¼ cup tamari
2 Tbsp lemon, lime, or orange juice
4 tsp hoisin sauce
1 Tbsp cornstarch
Sesame seeds, for garnish
Chopped spring onions, for garnish

STEAMED WHOLE FISH

Steeped in the symbolism of togetherness and unity, serving a steamed whole fish at important family gatherings is an age-old Chinese food tradition. The elders at the table were always given rights to claim the most covetable parts of the fish—the head, belly, and tail—but Mom always found a way to sneak me a fish cheek (the most tender part of the fish). I love using rockfish or bass for this dish.

Rinse fish under cold running water, then pat dry with a kitchen towel.

Bring water to a boil in a steamer. Place fish on a lipped heatproof plate, ensuring it lies flat and fully inside the plate, for even cooking. Sprinkle with half of the ginger and half of the spring onions. Season lightly with salt and pepper. Cover with plastic wrap and steam over high heat for 8–10 minutes until cooked through. (If a chopstick can easily pierce the fish, it's fully cooked.) Remove from heat.

Heat oil in a small frying pan over high heat. Add soy sauce (or tamari)—careful, it may splatter. Remove plastic wrap from fish and pour oil mixture over fish. Garnish with the remaining ginger and spring onions, cilantro and parsley.

Serve immediately with rice.

Make It Gluten-Free This dish can be made gluten-free by using tamari instead of soy sauce.

Serves 4

DF, QUICK
Prep 10 min
Cook 10–15 min

1 (1½–2-lb) whole white fish (I prefer rockfish), cleaned, head and tail on
2 slices ginger, cut into thin matchsticks (divided)
2 spring onions, sliced diagonally (divided)
Salt and black pepper to taste
3 Tbsp canola oil
2 Tbsp soy sauce or tamari (divided)
Sprig of cilantro, coarsely chopped
2 sprigs Italian parsley
Steamed rice, to serve

TAIWANESE SQUID

In many street markets, such as the night markets in Taiwan, you'll find food stands dedicated to whole grilled squid. Make this easy recipe the next time you fire up the BBQ.

Marinated squid In a bowl, combine ginger, spring onions, teriyaki marinade, salt, and pepper. Massage squid with the mixture, then let stand for at least 15 minutes.

Fill a large bowl with ice water. Bring a large saucepan of water to a boil. Carefully lower squid into the water and blanch for 15 seconds. Using a slotted spoon, immediately transfer squid to the ice bath to cool. Pat dry.

Using a sharp knife, score squid in a crosshatch pattern, taking care to not pierce entirely through the flesh.

Tamari sauce Vigorously whisk together all ingredients in a small bowl.

Mango salsa Preheat grill to 350°F.

Lightly brush oil over mango slices. Place mango on grill and sear for 2 minutes on each side. Transfer mango to a bowl, add the remaining ingredients, and stir to mix well.

Assembly Preheat grill to 350°F. Skewer whole squid lengthwise and brush sauce all over.

Place squid on the grill and cook for 5–6 minutes on each side. Brush more sauce on squid, then grill for another 4–5 minutes, turning half-way through cooking time.

Arrange frisée on a serving platter. Place squid on top, garnish with sesame seeds and cilantro, and serve with mango salsa.

Make It Gluten-Free This dish can be made gluten-free by using gluten-free teriyaki sauce.

Serves 2

DF
Prep 10 min,
plus 15 min standing time
Cook 20 min

Marinated squid
1½ Tbsp finely chopped ginger
1½ Tbsp finely chopped spring onions
3 Tbsp teriyaki marinade
Salt and black pepper to taste
1 lb squid, cleaned, membrane and head removed

Tamari sauce
¼ cup tamari
1½ Tbsp agave nectar
4 tsp rice wine vinegar

Mango salsa
1 semi-ripe mango (one fully ripe will be too soft), peeled and cut into large slices
1½ Tbsp olive oil
1 bird's eye chile, seeded, deveined, and chopped
1 small red onion, finely chopped
½ red bell pepper, seeded, deveined, and finely chopped
2 Tbsp finely chopped cilantro
1 Tbsp rice wine vinegar
1 tsp agave nectar

Assembly
10-inch wooden skewer
Marinated Squid (see here)
Tamari Sauce (see here)
Frisée, to serve
White sesame seeds, toasted
Chopped cilantro

THE NEW CANADIAN BEEF AND BARLEY

My mother landed first in Calgary when she arrived in Canada, so that city holds a special place in my heart. When Tourism Calgary asked me to help promote the city's culinary scene, I seized the opportunity to develop a recipe with two quintessential Albertan ingredients: beef and barley. Ingredients were sourced from local artisans, farmers, and in the historical Chinatown, then Charbar chef Connie DeSousa and I worked together to create our own interpretation of hearty and comforting Canadian classics.

Rice Place the ingredients in a sieve and thoroughly rinse under cold running water until the water runs clear. Transfer to a saucepan and add enough water to cover grains by 1 inch. Cook over medium-high heat, uncovered, for 8 minutes. Stir, then reduce heat to low. Cover and cook, stirring periodically, for another 10 minutes, until grains are nicely fluffed. (Alternatively, a rice cooker or Instant Pot is a convenient way to cook the grains.)

Beef Season beef with salt and pepper.

Heat oil in a large frying pan over high heat. Add beef and cook for 1–2 minutes on each side, until browned and the internal temperature reaches 130°F for medium-rare. Transfer beef to a plate lined with paper towel to drain and let rest for 15 minutes. (You can also sous-vide beef at 130°F for 1½ hours before searing, which allows for optimum flavour penetration and consistent cooking of the meat.)

Serves 4 (as an appetizer)

DF
Prep 20 min,
plus 15 min resting time
Cook 25 min

Rice
½ cup short-grain rice
¼ cup Alberta barley
¼ cup brown sweet rice
1 Tbsp black or purple rice

Beef
1 (10–12-oz) *Certified Angus Beef* striploin or flank
Salt and black pepper to taste
2 Tbsp canola oil

Chimichurri In a food processor, pulse all ingredients except lime juice until thoroughly combined. Stir in lime juice.

Assembly If desired, peel beets. Using a mandolin (use the guard!), slice beets, then chop into thin matchsticks. Place in a bowl and mix together.

Scoop rice onto one side of a plate and garnish with beet mixture and walnuts. Slice beef into thin pieces and fan on plate. Generously drizzle with chimichurri and garnish with micro greens. Serve immediately.

Chimichurri
5 mint leaves, finely chopped
2 spring onions, finely chopped
2 cloves garlic, finely chopped
1–2 bird's eye chiles, seeded, deveined, and finely chopped
½ cup finely chopped cilantro
¼ cup finely chopped Italian parsley
½ tsp black pepper
½ cup canola oil
¼ cup rice wine vinegar
¼ cup red wine vinegar
2 Tbsp sesame oil
Large pinch of coarse salt
Juice of 1 lime

Assembly
1 candy cane (Chioggia) beet, well rinsed
1 golden beet, well rinsed
Rice (see here)
½ cup crushed walnuts
Beef (see here)
Chimichurri (see here)
½ cup micro daikon radish, for garnish (see note)

The Message Micro daikon radish is commonly found at fine food stores, produce specialists, and farmers' markets.

THE NEW CANADIAN BEEF AND BARLEY (PAGE 122)

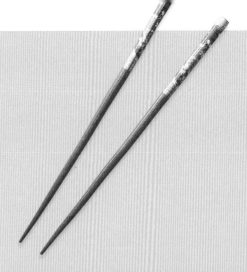

IT'S ALWAYS A FAMILY AFFAIR

According to one Chinese proverb, "food is bigger than the emperor," meaning that there is no greater importance than food itself. I myself can only think of a few things in life that bring as much happiness as eating good food and engaging in great conversations with friends and family. The connections and bonds made over meals are unlike anything else in this world.

What we eat is as important as how we eat it. The Chinese have developed strong dining traditions steeped in symbolism. At home, the ritual of dining is casual and convivial yet focused—I'm often impressed by the speed at which family members can simultaneously eat, pick up more food with their chopsticks, and chat. The meal begins with a soup to *hoi wai*, or "open up your soul" (generally, the only liquid served at a meal), then moves on to the main attraction: a variety of dishes laid out communally for everyone to help themselves from. They often include one or two meat or seafood dishes, a vegetable dish, and an equal amount of rice (or noodles, if you're from the north).

The Chinese believe that a harmonious dining experience involves contrasting tastes and textures, where bold dishes are paired with milder ones, or deep-fried dishes are complemented by steamed ones. According to the ancient Chinese philosopher Yi Yin, each of our taste sensations (sour, sweet, salty, bitter, and piquant) impacts one of the body's five major organ systems. Balance is seen as a way of maintaining good health.

I have always loved the shared experience of eating family-style and the notion that every seating is an opportunity to share stories and build new memories. Here are a few sample menus you might find at my table at home.

The Classic
Pork Bone Soup (page 107)
Chinese Meatloaf with Preserved Vegetables (*Jing Yuk Bang*) (page 99)
Mapo Tofu (page 131)
Chinese Okra and Mushroom Stir-Fry (page 129)
Steamed Rice

Clean and Lean
Egg Drop Soup (page 74)
Steamed Whole Fish (page 119)
Sesame Ginger Chicken (page 117)
Green Bean Baby (page 52)
Steamed Rice or Summer Tropical Rice (page 147)

Truly Canadian
Farm-Style Tuscan Soup (page 172)
The New Canadian Beef and Barley (page 122)
Three-Nations Chicken (page 92)
Kung Pao–Style Cauliflower Wings (page 57)
Red Rooster Fried Rice (page 146)
Coconut Chia Pudding with Minted Peach (page 67)

CHICKEN AND MUSHROOM STIR-FRY (MOO GOO GAI PAN)

Moo goo gai pan **translated from Cantonese means mushrooms and sliced chicken. With the option of using snow pea leaves— one of my favourite Asian greens—this is a modern take on the home-style dish.**

In a bowl, combine wine, cornstarch, soy sauce (or tamari), and 1 tablespoon water. Add chicken to the marinade, turning to coat. Cover and refrigerate for 30–45 minutes.

Heat oil in a frying pan over high heat. Add garlic and cook for 30 seconds, until fragrant. Add chicken and sauté for 6–7 minutes, until evenly cooked. If pan is slightly dry, add a tablespoon of water.

Stir in both mushrooms and sauté for 2–3 minutes. Add snow peas (or snow pea leaves) and stir-fry for 2–3 minutes, until bright green. Season with salt and pepper, remove from heat, then cover and let stand for 1 minute. Transfer to a serving platter and serve with rice.

Make It Gluten-Free This dish can be made gluten-free by using tamari instead of soy sauce.

Serves 4

DF
Prep 10 min, plus 30–45 min marinating time
Cook 15 min

1 Tbsp Chinese cooking wine (Shaoxing)
1 tsp cornstarch
½ tsp soy sauce or tamari
1½ chicken breasts, sliced into bite-sized pieces
2 Tbsp canola oil
1 clove garlic, finely chopped
1 cup sliced king oyster mushrooms
½ cup sliced shiitake mushrooms
2 cups snow peas, or snow pea leaves
⅓ tsp salt
⅓ tsp black pepper
Steamed rice, to serve

A TRIBE CALLED HAKKA

This traditional Hakka-style dish, native to Taiwan, was my most oft-eaten staff meal at Kanpai Snack Bar. It was perfect with a bowl of hot, fragrant white rice. Each bite explodes with flavour: a medley of saltiness, sweetness, and lingering heat on the finish.

Pour 1 cup hot water in a small bowl. Add mushrooms and soak for at least 1 hour. Remove mushrooms, reserving soaking liquid, then stem and cut into thin strips.

Heat ½ cup oil in a small saucepan over high heat. Using a metal slotted spoon, carefully lower pork belly into the oil and flash-fry for 2–3 minutes, until crisp and brown. Transfer to a plate lined with paper towel to drain.

Heat the remaining 2 tablespoons oil in a wok or frying pan over high heat. Add white onions, celery, and spring onions and sauté for 2 minutes, until vegetables are slightly softened. Add pork, tofu, and squid and sauté for 3–4 minutes. Stir in soy sauce (or tamari), chili oil, and sugar. Add a splash of the mushroom soaking liquid and increase heat to high. Add cooking wine and cook for another minute, until sauces are fully mixed and squid is cooked (it will firm and take form).

Transfer to a serving platter, then garnish with Thai basil leaves and chiles. Serve over rice.

The Message Chinese celery, a skinnier version of regular celery, has thin, hollow, and crunchy stalks and a strong flavour. It can be found at most Asian grocery stores.

Make It Gluten-Free This dish can be made gluten-free by using tamari instead of soy sauce.

Serves 2

DF
Prep 10 min, plus 1 hr soaking time
Cook 10 min

4–5 dried shiitake mushrooms, rinsed
½ cup + 2 Tbsp canola oil (divided)
2 oz pork belly, cut into ½-inch pieces
¼ white onion, thinly sliced
1 stalk Chinese celery, chopped (see note)
1 spring onion, chopped
1 oz marinated tofu, cut into thin strips
3–4 oz fresh or frozen squid, cut into rings
2 tsp soy sauce or tamari
2 tsp chili oil
1 tsp sugar
½ tsp Chinese cooking wine (Shaoxing)
2 Thai basil leaves, cut into thin strips, for garnish
1 bird's eye chile, finely chopped, for garnish
Steamed rice, to serve

CHINESE OKRA AND MUSHROOM STIR-FRY

It was on a location shoot for a *Cityline* segment that the line producer encouraged me to pick up a vegetable I had little experience cooking with, challenging me to work with Chinese okra. Somewhat of a misnomer, Chinese okra is not, in fact, an okra or even a vegetable, for that matter. The fruit is a relative of the cucumber and, when young, takes on a fresh, neutral taste.

Divide 3 cups hot water among 3 bowls. Soak pearl mushrooms, wood ear mushrooms, and lily buds separately for 1–2 hours. Reserve the pearl mushroom soaking liquid. Drain the liquid from wood ear mushrooms and lily buds.

Heat oil in a wok or pan over high heat. Add garlic and sauté for 1 minute, until fragrant. Add Chinese okra and bell peppers and stir-fry for 3–4 minutes, until softened and peppers are bright and crisp. Stir in mushrooms and lilies, tossing to mix. Reduce heat to medium.

Stir in oyster sauce, salt and pepper, ¼ cup water, and 3 tablespoons reserved pearl mushroom soaking liquid. Sauté mixture for 1–2 minutes, until bell peppers are al dente. Add chicken or pork (if using) and cook for another minute.

The Message Dried pearl (tiny oyster) mushrooms, wood ear mushrooms, and lily buds are common Chinese ingredients, used to add flavour, nutrients, and texture to dishes. They can be found in the dried food aisle of Asian supermarkets.

Chinese okra, also known as luffa or and *sing gua*, looks like a dull, longer version of an English cucumber. When stir-fried, the flavour is mild and sweet and it takes on a texture similar to that of zucchini. It can be found at Asian grocery stores.

Go Veg! This dish can be made vegetarian by leaving out the meat and using vegetarian oyster sauce.

Serves 4

DF
Prep 10 min,
plus 1–2 hr soaking time
Cook 10 min

¼ cup dried pearl mushrooms, rinsed (see note)
¼ cup dried wood ear mushrooms, rinsed (see note)
¼ cup dried lily buds, rinsed (see note)
1 Tbsp canola oil
1 clove garlic, chopped
1 cup Chinese okra, peeled and cut into 2-inch-square segments (see note)
½ red bell pepper, seeded, deveined, and cut into thin strips
1 Tbsp oyster sauce
Salt and black pepper to taste
1 cooked chicken breast or pork tenderloin, sliced (optional)
Steamed rice, to serve

MAPO TOFU

Anthony Bourdain professed his love for this dish during the Sichuan episode of *Anthony Bourdain: Parts Unknown*, and rightfully declared to Éric Ripert: "If you ever have a hangover—and you will, my friend, you will—this will scare the evil right out." When made right, this timeless dish of silky tofu, salty bean paste, and tongue-numbing chili peppers provides a perfectly well-balanced punch of flavours—it's a pleasure to eat every time.

In a small bowl, combine meat, 1 teaspoon soy sauce (or tamari), ¼ teaspoon sugar, and half of the garlic. Cover and refrigerate for 45–60 minutes.

Heat canola and sesame oils in a large frying pan over medium-high heat. Add peppercorns, then the remaining garlic. Add doubanjiang, chili oil, and stock, stirring until paste is fully dissolved. Add meat and cook for 5–6 minutes, stirring gently, until cooked through. Add the remaining ½ teaspoon sugar and 1 tablespoon soy sauce and bring mixture to a boil. Stir in tofu and lightly simmer for 2–3 minutes, until heated through.

Transfer to a platter and garnish with spring onions and chiles. Serve with rice.

Make It Gluten-Free This dish can be made gluten-free by using tamari instead of soy sauce.

Serves 3–4

DF

Prep 10 min, plus 45–60 min marinating time
Cook 10–15 min

5 oz ground pork, turkey, or chicken

5 tsp soy sauce or tamari (divided)

¾ tsp sugar (divided)

2 cloves garlic, finely chopped (divided)

1 Tbsp canola oil

1 tsp sesame oil

1 Tbsp slightly ground Szechuan peppercorns

3 Tbsp doubanjiang paste

2 tsp chili oil

1 cup vegetable stock

1 lb firm tofu, cut into ¾-inch cubes

1–2 spring onions, chopped, for garnish

2 bird's eye chiles, finely chopped, for garnish

Steamed rice, to serve

HONEY-GARLIC SPARE RIBS

I like to serve these delectable, easy-to-eat riblets with steamed rice, the perfect vessel for the super sticky, super tasty honey-garlic sauce. Trust me, it *is* the right thing to do.

Crispy garlic chips Heat oil in a small saucepan over medium-high heat. Carefully place garlic in the oil and deep-fry for 3–4 minutes, until golden and crispy. Using a slotted metal spoon, transfer to a plate lined with paper towel, to drain. Finely chop or pulse garlic chips. (Leftover garlic chips can be stored in an airtight container for up to 10 days.)

Honey-garlic spare ribs In a bowl, combine garlic, wine, vinegar, sugar, 3 tablespoons honey, and 1½ tablespoons water. Add riblets to the marinade, turning to coat. Cover and refrigerate for at least 8 hours.

Remove riblets from marinade, reserving marinade. In a clean bowl, stir riblets with cornstarch until no clumps remain. Put ribs in a colander and shake off any excess starch.

Heat oil in a deep fryer or deep saucepan over high heat to 350°F. Using a metal slotted spoon, gently lower riblets into the oil, working in batches to avoid overcrowding, and deep-fry for 4–5 minutes, until they are crispy and golden brown and float to the surface. Transfer riblets to a plate lined with paper towel to drain, then keep warm in the oven.

Simmer the reserved marinade in a medium saucepan over high heat. Reduce heat to low and simmer for 2–3 minutes, until marinade is reduced and thickened.

Transfer riblets to a bowl. Add half of the chiles, along with marinade. Toss riblets to coat.

Arrange riblets on a serving platter, then drizzle with the remaining 2 tablespoons honey. Sprinkle with crispy garlic chips and garnish with chiles.

Serves 6–8

DF, GF
Prep 20 min, plus 8 hr marinating time
Cook 25 min

Crispy garlic chips
1½ cups canola oil
1 head garlic, cloves separated and thinly sliced

Honey-garlic spare ribs
1 clove garlic, finely chopped
1½ Tbsp Chinese cooking wine (Shaoxing)
1½ Tbsp rice wine vinegar
1 Tbsp brown sugar
5 Tbsp local honey (divided)
1¼ lbs pork spare ribs, cut into bite-sized pieces (ask your butcher)
½ cup cornstarch
3 cups canola oil
2 bird's eye chiles, finely chopped (divided)
2 Tbsp Crispy Garlic Chips (see here), for garnish

GINGER-GREEN TEA BEEF WITH CILANTRO-GINGER AIOLI AND CRISPY NOODLES

I created this recipe for a client who wanted a curated tea experience. I assembled a series of unique Chinese teas, and accompanied them with this dish involving various components. This recipe makes for a great dinner starter or cocktail hors d'oeuvre (serve on Chinese soup spoons) when prepared in smaller portions.

Ginger-green tea beef Bring 1½ cups water to a boil in a small saucepan. Add tea bags, turn off heat, and steep, covered, for 10 minutes. Remove bags and let tea cool.

In a bowl large enough to fit the steak, combine all ingredients except tea and steak. Pour in tea and, using a fork, mix thoroughly. Add beef to the marinade, turning to coat. Cover and refrigerate for 12 hours.

Cilantro-ginger aioli In a food processor, pulse all ingredients except mayonnaise. Transfer to a serving bowl and carefully fold in mayonnaise, then cover and refrigerate until ready to use.

Serves 4–6

DF

Prep 10 min, plus 10 min steeping time, 12 hr marinating time, and 10 min resting time

Cook 20 min

Ginger-green tea beef
4 bags green tea
2 spring onions, chopped
2 cloves garlic, finely chopped
2–3 sprigs cilantro, coarsely chopped
2 Tbsp chopped ginger
2 Tbsp canola oil
3 Tbsp soy sauce or tamari
3 Tbsp brown sugar or maple syrup
Pinch of salt
Pinch of black pepper
1 (1-lb) *Certified Angus Beef* high-grade flank steak

Cilantro-ginger aioli
Sprig of cilantro, hand torn
2 Tbsp finely chopped ginger
1 Tbsp canola oil
¼ tsp salt
Pinch of black pepper
Juice of ½ lime
¼ cup mayonnaise

Assembly
Ginger–Green Tea Beef (see here)
2 cups + 2 tsp canola oil (divided)
Cilantro-Ginger Aioli (see here)
4 oz chow mein egg noodles
Choice of micro greens,
    for garnish

Assembly Remove beef from marinade, then pat dry.

Heat 2 cups oil in a deep saucepan over high heat to 375°F. Gently lower in noodles and fry for 3–4 minutes, until crisp. Transfer to a plate lined with paper towel to drain and let cool.

Preheat oven to 275°F.

Heat the remaining 2 teaspoons oil in a large ovenproof frying pan over high heat. Add beef and sear for 2 minutes on each side, until lightly charred at the edges. Transfer pan to oven and cook for 10 minutes. Remove pan from oven, transfer beef to a plate, and let rest for 10 minutes.

Thinly slice beef on a bias. Scoop a spoonful of aioli into the centre of 4–6 plates. Place crispy noodles on the aioli, then arrange 3–4 slices of beef over the noodles. Garnish with micro greens and serve immediately.

GINGER-GREEN TEA BEEF WITH CILANTRO-
GINGER AIOLI AND CRISPY NOODLES (PAGE 134)

THE CHRONIC: I'M HOOKED AND I WANT TO DO MORE

When I started cooking again in 2014, I loved watching people enjoy my food—just as my grandfather did at Highbell—and I relished the creative outlet I had in the kitchen or with my notebook, writing new recipes. There was something addictive about wearing a suit during the day and donning an apron at night. And I wanted more of it.

It was time to bring something new and tasty to the world—and instead of tearing down my eatery at the end of each day, it would need to be something more permanent. Through a lucky break, I was given the chance to put my mark on the city of Toronto with a new emerging cuisine and a restaurant serving up Taiwanese street food, the hip-hop way. (Kanpai was going to be the start of something great.)

Just like my grandfather did before me, I spun one of the most iconic North American dishes into Asian fusion gold: Taiwanese Fried Chicken, served the southern way with a little bit of hip-hop swag. It was time to get everyone else hooked.

I continued to obsess over unique and wonderful dishes when I opened my next venture at the Food Building at The Ex, an iconic summertime stop for anyone who grew up in Toronto. (Once known for its 25-cent hot dogs, The Ex was then on the verge of becoming a renewed hub for culinary innovation.) I partnered to create Yatai, a food joint that served up riffs on Japanese street eats, such as the ramen burger—a juicy beef patty nestled between two ramen buns (page 102)—to hungry patrons.

I didn't see the success coming, but when the doors opened, people came. My perception of food and dining changed forever that summer, and the public's reaction to the food inspired me to reach further and create more.

粉麵飯

RICE & NOODLES

MEIN STREETS

When it comes to Chinese food, noodles are arguably as important as rice, and often far more symbolic than most people realize. Representing longevity or long life, noodles are always served at special occasions, near the end of the meal. There are so many variations! Here are a few of my favourites.

chow mein egg noodles These thin egg noodles are often used in stir-fry noodle dishes—and whenever you want the noodles to be crispy. They can be substituted with thin wonton noodles, but be sure to first boil those in water for a minute until just tender. Use in Ginger–Green Tea Beef with Cilantro-Ginger Aioli and Crispy Noodles (page 134), Cantonese Chow Mein (page 160), and The Last Samurai (page 102).

ho fun Also known as chow fun noodles, these flat, wide rice noodles are common in South China, where they are used in stir-fry noodle or soup recipes. Use in Hong Kong–Style Curry Rice Noodles (page 156).

mung bean vermicelli Mung bean vermicelli are dried, white, and thin noodles, closely resembling rice vermicelli. Use in Chilled Noodles (page 163).

ramen It's been said that the first ramen shop, named Rairaiken, was opened in Tokyo in 1910 by a Japanese owner, who employed twelve Cantonese cooks to serve the ramen. The term itself is a Japanese transcription of the Chinese word *lamian*. Fresh ramen is yellow, thin, and very long, with a toothsome texture. It is available either fresh in bags (at Asian food stores) or dried in plastic or cellophane packs. Use in Ramen with L.A. Kalbi (page 164).

Shanghai noodles With a good chew, these thick, creamy-coloured, hearty noodles are ideal for stir-fries. They are available fresh or dried. Use in Sunday Shanghai Noodles (page 159).

sweet potato glass noodles Also known as cellophane or glass noodles, these noodles are generally made with potato starch and served in various ways across Asia (in Korea, they're used in *japchae*, a sweet and savoury stir-fry dish). They come in both thin and wide versions. Use in Chilled Noodles (page 163).

udon These thick, white, chewy wheat noodles from Japan tend to be served hot in soupy dishes but also make for a good stir-fry. They are available precooked and vacuum-packed. Before use, pour boiling water in a bowl, then add the noodles to refresh for 2–3 minutes. Use in Ramen with L.A. Kalbi (page 164).

wonton noodles, thin These thin, springy egg noodles are perfect for wonton noodle soup. They're often boiled, drained, and then served with a sizzling oil or sauce on top. These noodles don't require much cooking time—about 30–40 seconds—so be mindful of the cooking time to ensure an ideal texture. Use in Ramen with L.A. Kalbi (page 164).

ho fun

chow mein egg noodles

sweet potato
glass noodles

mung bean
vermicelli

ramen

Shanghai noodles

udon

wonton noodles, thin

PINEAPPLE FRIED RICE

The first time I can remember eating this dish was at the Lui family reunion in Hong Kong, when I was four years old. I was awestruck when I saw the servers march into the restaurant with the pineapples. Years later, I provided a recipe for this dish for a publication featuring unique holiday dishes.

With a paring knife, remove pineapple flesh, keeping the top and half shell intact. Core pineapple and cut into ¾-inch cubes. Wipe and pat dry the hollowed pineapple half.

Heat 1 tablespoon oil in a wok or large skillet over high heat. Add egg and scramble for 1–2 minutes, until just cooked through. Transfer to a cutting board and chop into pieces.

Heat the remaining 3 tablespoons oil in the same pan over high heat. Add peas, bell peppers, and both onions and cook for 3 minutes until onions are translucent. Stir in ham (or pork) and cook for another 2 minutes. Stir in rice, folding constantly to ensure rice does not stick to the pan. Sprinkle a few drops of water into rice to hydrate and loosen any clumps. Stir in egg. Season with salt and pepper.

Transfer rice to hollowed pineapple shell. Garnish with cilantro and serve with a side of chili oil.

The Message Did you know that *the* best fried rice is made with day-old rice? When cooked rice is chilled, it becomes dehydrated, and the grains loosen and separate easily when it's recooked (reducing clumping). Sprinkle water over the rice as you are frying it, to slowly rehydrate it and create the perfect consistency.

Serves 2

DF, GF, QUICK
Prep 10 min
Cook 10 min

½ pineapple, cut lengthwise and top intact
4 Tbsp vegetable or canola oil (divided)
1 egg
⅓ cup peas
¼ red bell pepper, diced
⅓ cup chopped red onions
⅓ cup chopped spring onions
¾ cup chopped ham or diced cooked pork
3 cups day-old cooked jasmine rice (see note)
⅓ tsp salt
Black pepper to taste
Sprig of cilantro, for garnish
Chili oil, to serve

RED ROOSTER FRIED RICE

This popular rice dish at Kanpai seemingly flew from our woks onto everyone's tables. Not just any fried rice, this one is loaded with flavour thanks to the savoury and spicy combo. The name "Red Rooster" is a play on the dish's colour and an ode to one of the Chinese zodiac signs. Turned out, it was a perfect accompaniment to my award-winning fried chicken (page 83).

Heat 2 tablespoons canola oil in a large wok or frying pan over high heat. Add meat and flash-fry for 2 minutes, until nearly cooked through. Transfer to a plate lined with paper towel to drain.

Heat the remaining 2 tablespoons oil in the same pan over high heat. Crack an egg into the pan and scramble it for 1 minute, until just cooked through. Transfer to a plate.

In the same pan, place rice, bell peppers, and spring onions and sauté for 2–3 minutes, until vegetables have softened. Stir in meat and sauté for another 2 minutes.

Add chili oil with black bean, chili oil, soy sauce (or tamari), sugar, and salt and sauté for 1 minute, until rice grains are loose and separated. (If rice is clumpy, flatten with a spatula. If rice appears dry or sticks to the pan, sprinkle with a little water.) Add chiles and toss. Transfer to a platter and serve.

The Message Lao Gan Ma's chili oil with black bean is a condiment made with fermented black soybeans (*douchi*) and often used in stir-fries or served with rice, noodles, or eggs. It can be found at Asian supermarkets.

Did you know that the best fried rice is made with day-old rice? When cooked rice is chilled, it becomes dehydrated, and the grains loosen and separate easily when it's recooked (reducing clumping). Sprinkle water over the rice as you are frying it, to slowly rehydrate it and create the perfect consistency.

Make It Gluten-Free This dish can be made gluten-free by using tamari instead of soy sauce.

Serves 2

DF, QUICK
Prep 10 min
Cook 10 min

4 Tbsp canola oil (divided)

3 oz pork loin, chicken thigh, or *Certified Angus Beef* flank, cut into strips

1 egg

1½ cups day-old cooked jasmine rice, chilled (see note)

¼ red bell pepper, seeded, deveined, and chopped

1 spring onion, chopped

2 Tbsp Lao Gan Ma's chili oil with black bean (see note)

1 Tbsp chili oil

1 Tbsp soy sauce or tamari

1 tsp sugar

½ tsp salt

1 bird's eye chile, seeded, deveined, and finely chopped

SUMMER TROPICAL RICE

A staple in Asian restaurants and households, this easy-to-execute dish is a great alternative to plain rice. The addition of a few sunny island flavours transforms this delicious dish into an enjoyable midweek meal for the entire family.

In a saucepan, bring wild rice, ¼ teaspoon salt, and 2 cups water to a boil. Cover, reduce heat to medium-low, and cook for 45 minutes, until rice is chewy and some of the grains have burst.

In a separate saucepan, bring brown (or basmati) rice, the remaining ¼ teaspoon salt, and 2 cups water to a boil. Cover, reduce heat to medium-low, and cook for 30–40 minutes, until rice is cooked through.

Transfer both rice mixtures to a large bowl and let cool to room temperature.

Add oil and mix well to coat rice. Pour in coconut milk and mix again. Stir in ginger and spring onions, and season with salt and pepper.

Serves 4

DF, GF, VEG
Prep 10 min
Cook 1½ hr

½ cup wild rice, rinsed well
½ tsp salt, plus extra to taste (divided)
1 cup brown or basmati rice, rinsed well
1 Tbsp canola oil
¼ cup coconut milk
2 Tbsp finely chopped ginger
2 Tbsp finely chopped spring onions
Black pepper to taste

RAJMA CHAWAL

Rajma chawal is a popular Indian vegetarian dish of red kidney beans stewed in a spicy gravy and served with rice—it is arguably my wife's favourite dish. Although we serve this delicious version frequently at home, it's true what they say: nothing is ever as good as Mom's.

Bring 4 cups water to a boil in a medium saucepan. Add beans, garlic, and salt and cook for 10–12 minutes, until beans are softened. Reduce to low heat, cover, and simmer for 6–7 minutes.

Heat oil in a saucepan over high heat. Add onions and cumin seeds and sauté for 3–4 minutes, until onions are brown and softened. Stir in fenugreek, garam masala, chili powder, turmeric, and tomato paste. Reduce heat to medium and sauté for 3–4 minutes, until fragrant. Stir in kidney bean mixture and reduce heat to low. Cover and simmer for 12 minutes.

Serve over basmati rice.

Serves 2–4

DF, GF, VEG
Prep 10 min
Cook 40 min

2 cups canned red kidney beans
4 cloves garlic, finely chopped
1 tsp salt
¼ cup canola oil
1 white onion, finely chopped
1½ tsp cumin seeds
2 Tbsp fenugreek
1 tsp garam masala
1 tsp red chili powder
½ tsp ground turmeric
2 Tbsp tomato paste
Steamed basmati rice, to serve

BAKED PORK CHOP OVER RICE (*GUK JUI PA FAN*)

If there was ever a quintessential Hong Kong dish, this might be it. Found in many cafés and congee-noodle houses, no matter where they are, it's generally eaten at lunch or for afternoon tea (often with a cup of hot milk tea). Grandpa TK's has a special place in my heart and, in my unbiased opinion, I have yet to taste one that comes close to his. At the restaurant, he made this dish every few weeks as a special staff meal.

Pork chops In a bowl, combine 2 tablespoons oil, soy sauce (or tamari), wine, pepper, cornstarch, and ¼ cup water. Add pork chops to the marinade, turning to coat. Cover and refrigerate for 45–60 minutes.

Heat the remaining 2½ tablespoons oil in a frying pan over high heat. Add pork chops and pan-fry for 4–5 minutes on each side, until golden brown. Transfer to a plate lined with paper towel to drain.

Fried rice Heat oil in a wok or frying pan over high heat. Add eggs and scramble until nearly cooked through. Add rice and season with salt and pepper. Sprinkle rice with 2 teaspoons water if it appears dry. Stir in peas and corn and cook until warmed through. Keep warm.

Tomato sauce In a food processor, pulse all ingredients and ½ cup water, until smooth. Pour sauce into a saucepan and bring to a boil over high heat. Reduce heat to medium and simmer for 3–4 minutes. Set aside.

Assembly Preheat oven to 350°F.

Scoop fried rice into a 9- × 13-inch baking dish and level it with a wooden spoon. Add pork chops, then top with tomato sauce. Bake for 15 minutes, until sauce begins to bubble. Bake for another 5 minutes, until sauce is caramelized. Remove from heat and let cool for 5 minutes before serving.

Serves 4

DF
Prep 20 min, plus 45–60 min marinating time
Cook 45 min

Pork chops
4½ Tbsp canola oil (divided)
1½ tsp soy sauce or tamari
1½ tsp Chinese cooking wine (Shaoxing)
½ tsp white pepper
3 Tbsp cornstarch
4 boneless pork chops

Fried rice
1 Tbsp canola oil
2 eggs, beaten
4 cups day-old jasmine rice (see note)
Salt and black pepper to taste
½ cup peas
½ cup corn kernels

Tomato sauce
1 (28-oz) can stewed tomatoes
1 Tbsp ketchup
2 tsp sugar
1 tsp white vinegar
1 tsp soy sauce or tamari

The Message Did you know that the best fried rice is made with day-old rice? When cooked rice is chilled, it becomes dehydrated, and the grains loosen and separate easily creating the perfect texture.

Make It Gluten-Free This dish can be made gluten-free by using tamari instead of soy sauce.

TANDOORI MASALA CHICKEN FRIED RICE

When combined, Chinese fried rice and classic Indian seasonings take on the flavours of indigenous Hakka cuisine. This comforting dish is a cultural nod and homage to the Tangra region of Kolkata, India, where Hakka-Chinese cuisine originated.

Tandoori masala chicken Heat 1½ tablespoons oil in a large frying pan over high heat. Add curry leaves and flash-fry for 1–2 minutes, until leaves crisp up.

In a bowl, stir curry leaves with cilantro, tandoori seasoning, tamari, and cinnamon. Add chicken to the marinade, stirring to coat. Cover and refrigerate for at least 2 hours but preferably 8 hours.

Heat the remaining 1½ tablespoons oil in a wok or frying pan over high heat. Add chicken mixture and sauté for 5–6 minutes, until cooked through.

Fried rice Heat 3 tablespoons oil in the same frying pan over medium-high heat. Add egg and scramble for 1–2 minutes, until just slightly undercooked. Transfer to a small plate.

Heat the remaining 3 tablespoons oil in the frying pan over medium-high heat. Add both onions, carrots, and peas and cook for 4–5 minutes, until onions are translucent. Stir in rice, folding constantly to prevent it from sticking to the pan. Add tandoori masala chicken and egg, then season with salt and pepper.

Transfer mixture to a serving platter and garnish with cilantro and chiles (if using).

Serves 2

DF, GF
Prep 10 min, plus at least 2 hr marinating time
Cook 15 min

Tandoori masala chicken
3 Tbsp vegetable or canola oil (divided)
Sprig of curry leaves, leaves only
¼ cup chopped cilantro
1½ Tbsp tandoori masala seasoning
1 Tbsp tamari
½ tsp ground cinnamon
2 chicken breasts, cut into 1-inch cubes

Fried rice
6 Tbsp vegetable or canola oil (divided)
1 egg
1 spring onion, finely chopped
½ small red onion, finely chopped
½ small carrot, finely chopped
⅓ cup fresh or frozen peas
2½ cups day-old cooked jasmine or basmati rice (see note)
Salt and black pepper to taste
Cilantro, coarsely chopped, for garnish
Bird's eye chile, seeded and chopped, for garnish (optional)

The Message Did you know that the best fried rice is made with day-old rice? When cooked rice is chilled, it becomes dehydrated, and the grains loosen and separate easily creating the perfect texture.

HARVEST GRAIN CONGEE WITH ONSEN TAMAGO

I've spent countless hours in the kitchen developing a healthy and nourishing congee (rice porridge), with all the sustenance and wholesome flavours of the classic dish I grew up with. The harvest grain congee debuted to hundreds of taste testers at a national culinary tradeshow and, later, became the fastest-selling dish at a soup festival.

Pour 1 cup warm water into a small bowl. Add mushrooms and soak for 1 hour. Remove mushrooms, reserving soaking liquid (you'll need about ¾ cup), then stem mushrooms and finely chop.

Combine rice, quinoa, and lentils in a colander and rinse thoroughly. Transfer to a stockpot and add garlic and ginger. Pour in 16 cups water and bring mixture to a boil over high heat. Reduce heat to medium, then add chili flakes and season with salt and pepper. Partially cover and simmer for 20–30 minutes, stirring occasionally, until rice is broken. Season with salt and pepper. Reduce heat to low, cover pot tightly, and cook mixture for another 5 minutes. Turn off heat and stir.

Onsen tamago With a sous-vide in a water bath, set water temperature to 147°F. Add eggs and cook for 47 minutes. Remove and let cool. When cracked open, whites should be milky and yolk should be whole but slightly runny inside. (Alternatively, a soft poach or a 7-minute soft-boiled egg works just as well.)

Assembly Ladle congee into 8 bowls. Carefully break open eggs, discarding excess egg white (the runny egg white will have separated from the yolk. The yolk will be a perfect sphere, covered with a thin layer of cooked egg white.) Gently place yolks on congee. Finish with your favourite toppings and serve.

Serves 8

DF, GF, VEG
Prep 10 min, plus 1 hr soaking time
Cook 1½ hr

6 dried shiitake mushrooms, rinsed
½ cup brown rice
½ cup red quinoa
½ cup green and red lentil blend
3 cloves garlic, finely chopped
1 Tbsp finely chopped ginger
½ tsp smoked red chili flakes
Salt and black pepper to taste

Onsen tamago
8 eggs

Toppings
Chili oil
Chopped cilantro
Chopped spring onions
Fried garlic chips
Furikake
Lime wedges
Pea shoots
White pepper

SUNDAY CONGEE

Congee is the one dish that "takes" me home, triggering every sense when it hits the table. Like Italian Sunday sugo, or the cornbread and collards of the Deep South, congee is Chinese "soul food"—especially when prepared alongside a plate of noodles (cue Mom's Sunday Shanghai Noodles, page 159). It's a simple dish that requires a little love and patience; the essence of my most cherished family meal resides in this dish. And to this day I still enjoy it at least once a week.

In a small bowl, combine pork, salt, and pepper. Cover and refrigerate for 1 hour.

In a large saucepan, thoroughly rinse rice under cold running water until water runs clear. Drain, then add 5 cups water and bring to a boil. Add pork and reduce heat to medium. Cover partially (to prevent air from being trapped and rice from boiling over) and simmer for 1½ hours, stirring occasionally to prevent rice from sticking to the bottom of the pan. Consistency is a personal preference: if you prefer the congee to be thinner, add more water to loosen it.

Cut duck egg into small cubes (be careful to not separate the yolk from the outer layer) and add to the congee. Reduce heat to low and simmer for 20–30 minutes, until rice is fully broken and there is no separation between rice and water. (Again, if the congee is too thin for your liking, add a little water.) Simmer for 2–3 minutes.

Ladle congee into individual bowls or a large serving bowl and garnish with ginger and spring onions. Season with white pepper.

The Message Asian grocers generally stock two types of duck eggs: a salted version and a preserved version. Be sure to use a preserved egg in this recipe, and remove the coating and wash the egg before cracking the shell. The preservation process gives the egg its charcoal colour.

Congee is often served with savoury doughnut fritters, which can be purchased at some bakeries or noodle shops.

Serves 4

DF, GF
Prep 10 min, plus 1 hr resting time
Cook 2 hr

⅔ lb pork shoulder, cut into 2-inch chunks

½ tsp salt

½ tsp white pepper, plus extra to taste

½ cup short-grain rice

1 preserved duck egg, peeled and rinsed (see note)

2 slices ginger, cut into thin strips, for garnish

1 spring onion, finely chopped, for garnish

TALK DOESN'T COOK RICE

Nothing sings to my heart quite like a bowl of congee. Uber-comforting and nourishing, the rice porridge can be served plain or loaded with additional flavours and toppings. Simply prepare the basic congee recipe—the Sunday Congee (page 154) or Harvest Grain Congee (page 152)—then add whatever ingredients suit your mood and simmer until the protein is cooked through. Finish it off with your favourite toppings and enjoy a bowl of soothing comfort. If you dine at a classic Chinese noodle and rice restaurant, you will generally find on offer a full menu section dedicated to the many variations of congee. Here are four suggestions.

Chicken and Mushroom Congee
2 Tbsp grated ginger
3 cloves grated garlic
2–5 dried shiitake mushrooms, soaked
2 cups skinless, boneless chicken thighs, cut into bite-sized pieces
2 cups baby bok choy, chopped

Seafood Congee
2 Tbsp grated ginger
3 dried scallops, soaked
2 cups fresh or frozen seafood of your choice

Ginger-Chicken Congee
½ cup shredded ginger
2 cups skinless, boneless chicken thighs, cut into bite-sized pieces

Minced Beef Congee
8 oz *Certified Angus Beef* ground chuck
5 cloves garlic, chopped
4 spring onions, chopped

Toppings
Century duck eggs
Chili oil
Cilantro
Crispy garlic
Crispy shallots
Dried shrimp
Eggs, hard-boiled or poached
Garlic chives
Ginger
Lime wedges
Peanuts
Salted duck eggs
Scallions
Shredded iceberg lettuce

HONG KONG–STYLE CURRY RICE NOODLES (*CHAR KWAY TEOW*)

This is my go-to whenever I hit the local noodle houses. The origins of this classic dish are rooted in Malaysia and Singapore, but the adapted version, found in Hong Kong noodle houses, is equally delicious.

Bring a large saucepan of water to a boil. Add noodles and blanch for 2 minutes. Drain, then rinse under cold running water and drain again.

Heat 1 tablespoon oil in a non-stick frying pan over high heat. Add eggs and scramble until cooked through. Transfer to a plate.

Heat the remaining 3 tablespoons oil in the same pan over medium-high heat. Add white onions and bell peppers and sauté for 5 minutes, until onions are slightly translucent. Add shrimp and pork and sauté for 3–4 minutes, until shrimp is opaque and cooked through. Add spring onions and noodles and stir-fry for 1 minute. Stir in soy sauce (or tamari), curry powder, chili oil, and pepper and cook for another minute. Stir in eggs and sprouts and sauté for 1 minute.

Transfer to a serving platter and serve immediately.

Make It Gluten-Free This dish can be made gluten-free by using tamari instead of soy sauce.

Serves 2–4

DF, QUICK
Prep 10 min
Cook 15 min

1 (23-oz) package precooked ho fun (chow fun) noodles
4 Tbsp canola oil (divided)
2 eggs
½ white onion, thinly sliced
½ red bell pepper, seeded, deveined, and cut into thin strips
8 shrimp, shelled and deveined
5½ oz BBQ pork (*char siu*)
2 spring onions, cut into strips
2 Tbsp soy sauce or tamari
2 tsp curry powder
1 tsp chili oil
½ tsp black pepper
½ cup bean sprouts

CARBONARA RAMEN

Some of the most prized dishes of my career have been serendipitous discoveries. On one occasion, I was testing take-out noodles for a new concept and had sous-vide eggs (*onsen tamago*) on hand. I added them to the container of noodles—the resulting silky yolk-coated noodles reminded me of carbonara. I debuted this dish at a private demo during a sake festival, and the reaction to it affirmed that it is something special. This carbonara-style *mazemen* (dry ramen) is meant to be eaten at just above room temperature.

With a sous-vide in a water bath, set water temperature to 147°F. Add eggs and cook for 47 minutes. Remove and let cool. (Alternatively, a soft poach or a 7-minute soft-boiled egg works just as well.)

Combine soy sauce (or tamari) and ponzu in a small saucepan and keep warm over medium-low heat.

Cut mushrooms into thin strips. Melt butter in a small frying pan over medium-high heat. Add mushrooms and sauté for 2–3 minutes, until cooked through. Season lightly with salt and pepper. Transfer to a plate.

Carefully break open eggs. The whites should be milky and yolk should be whole but slightly runny inside. Separate the egg yolk and discard the white.

Bring a large saucepan of water to a boil over high heat. Add noodles and cook until al dente. Drain, then rinse under cold running water. Divide noodles between 2 bowls. Ladle half of the ponzu mixture into each bowl. Arrange spring onions, mushrooms, and egg yolk on top of the noodles.

Sprinkle furikake and togarashi over the egg, then sprinkle with cheese. When you are ready to eat, puncture the egg and coat the noodles with the yolk. Serve immediately.

Serves 2

VEG
Prep 20 min
Cook 50 min

2 eggs
2 Tbsp soy sauce or tamari
2 Tbsp ponzu (see note)
8–10 wood ear mushrooms, soaked in warm water
1 Tbsp butter
Salt and black pepper to taste
1 lb dried ramen noodles
½ spring onion, chopped
Furikake, for garnish
Togarashi, for garnish
¼ cup finely grated Parmesan or Asiago

The Message Ponzu is a Japanese condiment with tart, citrus-based notes. Use it with or without soy sauce. It can be found at Asian supermarkets.

SUNDAY SHANGHAI NOODLES

Mom occasionally prepared large batches of Shanghai noodles to last us a couple days (unless I got my hands on them, that is). More often than not, she served them with congee (page 154)—my all-time favourite home-cooked Sunday meal. The thick Shanghai noodles have a bucatini-like thickness that holds sauce perfectly.

Bring water to a boil in a saucepan over high heat. Add noodles and cook for 2–3 minutes, until softened. Drain in a colander, then rinse under cold running water.

Heat 2 tablespoons oil in a large wok or frying pan over high heat. Add pork and stir-fry for 2–3 minutes, until browned and cooked through. Transfer to a plate.

To the same pan, add cabbage and spring onions and sauté in the residual pork fat for 3–4 minutes, until cabbage is cooked through. Add the remaining 2 tablespoons oil and noodles and stir-fry for 5–6 minutes, making sure the noodles do not stick. Stir in pork.

Stir in oyster sauce, soy sauce (or tamari), sugar, pepper, and ¼ cup water. Cover pan and cook for 20 seconds. Toss ingredients one last time.

Transfer to a serving platter and garnish with micro greens. Serve with sweet chili sauce on the side.

Serves 2–4

DF, QUICK
Prep 10 min
Cook 20 min

1 (20-oz) package thick Shanghai noodles
4 Tbsp canola oil (divided)
7 oz pork loin, cut into thin strips
½ small green cabbage, shredded
2 spring onions, cut into thin strips
2 Tbsp oyster sauce
1 Tbsp soy sauce or tamari
½ tsp sugar
½ tsp black pepper
½ cup micro greens (daikon radish, tatsoy, or mizuna work well), for garnish
Sweet chili sauce, for dipping

CANTONESE CHOW MEIN

Chow mein, or "fried noodles," comes in so many forms, but this version at the family restaurant, Highbell, was popular among the locals.

Bring a large saucepan of water to a boil. Add noodles and cook for 2 minutes, then drain in a colander and rinse under cold running water.

Bring a small saucepan of water to a boil. Add snow peas and cook for 2 minutes. Drain, then rinse under cold running water.

Heat 2 tablespoons oil in a large frying pan over high heat. Add noodles and pan-fry, untouched, for 3–4 minutes, until crisp. Turn over and pan-fry, untouched, for another 3–4 minutes, until crisp and slightly browned. (Note: the centre of the noodles can remain soft, if desired.) Transfer noodles to a serving platter.

Heat the remaining 2 tablespoons oil in the same pan over medium-high heat. Add carrots and yellow onions and sauté for 3–4 minutes, until onions are slightly translucent. Add shrimp and BBQ pork and sauté for another 3 minutes, until shrimp turns just opaque.

Add spring onions and snow peas and cook for a minute. Stir in soy sauce (or tamari), oyster sauce, and ½ cup water. Bring mixture to a simmer.

In a small bowl, combine cornstarch and 3 tablespoons water. Add cornstarch mixture to the pan, a tablespoon at a time, and stir until thick enough to coat the back of a wooden spoon. If necessary, add more cornstarch mixture.

Pour sauce over noodles, then garnish with cilantro and serve immediately, with chili oil (or sauce) on the side.

Serves 2

DF, QUICK
Prep 15 min
Cook 20 min

1 lb chow mein egg noodles
½ cup snow peas
4 Tbsp canola oil (divided)
½ carrot, thinly sliced diagonally
½ yellow onion, thinly sliced
6 (31/40) shrimp, shelled and deveined
5½ oz sliced BBQ pork (*char siu*)
2 spring onions, cut into matchsticks
1 Tbsp soy sauce or tamari
1 Tbsp oyster sauce
1 Tbsp cornstarch
Chopped cilantro, for garnish
Chili oil or sauce, to serve

Go Veg! This dish can be made vegetarian by omitting the meat and seafood and using vegetarian oyster sauce.

CHILLED NOODLES (*LIANG MEIN*)

When I was a child, my mom would prepare large batches of these noodles and leave them in the fridge for me to snack on. Traditionally, she used a wheat noodle called *yi mein* (also known as longevity noodles), but I've since adapted the recipe using a healthier, gluten-free alternative. It may resemble a chilled Korean noodle dish, but it is deeply rooted in Hong Kong flavours.

Bring a saucepan of salted water to a boil. Add noodles and cook according to package directions until al dente (about 5 minutes). Drain, then rinse under cold running water. If using sweet potato glass noodles, cut them in half. Place in a large mixing bowl.

Squeeze out any excess water and remove any seeds from the cucumber. Place cucumber, carrots, and spring onions in a bowl. Stir in black vinegar, oyster and hoisin sauces, and soy sauce (or tamari), mixing well.

Stir in both oils and mix well to coat noodles. Season with salt and pepper, then cover and refrigerate for at least 2 hours or overnight to chill. Garnish with sesame seeds and nori.

Make It Gluten-Free This dish can be made gluten-free by using tamari instead of soy sauce.

Serves 4

DF
Prep 10 min, plus at least 2 hr chilling time
Cook 5 min

1 (12-oz) package sweet potato (glass) noodles or yi mein
1 cucumber, seeded and cut into thin strips
1 carrot, cut into thin strips
2 spring onions, cut into thin strips
5½ oz cooked ham, cut into thin strips
3 Tbsp Chinese black vinegar
2 Tbsp oyster sauce
1 Tbsp hoisin sauce
1 Tbsp soy sauce or tamari
2 tsp canola oil
1 tsp sesame oil
½ tsp salt
½ tsp black pepper
½ tsp black and white sesame seeds, for garnish
2 Tbsp shredded nori, for garnish

RAMEN WITH L.A. KALBI

My daughter Lil' C has had a lifelong love for noodles of almost any kind, but it's ramen that she would eat every night if she could. And like her old man, she is a massive fan of Korean BBQ short ribs (also known as kalbi). When I asked her what favourite recipe of hers to include in the book, it was a toss-up. I had no choice but to roll them up into one big bowl to create for her the ultimate meal. Lil' C, I hope you are okay with this!

Marinated short ribs Put ½ cup water and all ingredients except ribs in a bowl and mix thoroughly to combine. Add ribs, cover, and refrigerate for 24 hours.

Ramen with L.A. kalbi Preheat oven to 350°F.

Heat oil on a grill or in a pan over medium-high heat. Remove ribs from the marinade and place on the grill. Sear for 3–4 minutes on each side, until ribs are caramelized.

Transfer to a baking sheet and bake for 6–8 minutes.

Bring a large saucepan of water to a boil over high heat. Add noodles and cook according to package directions until nearly al dente. Drain, then rinse under cold running water. Divide noodles between 2 bowls.

Ladle hot stock over noodles, until nearly all are submerged. Portion kalbi on one side of each bowl. Add fish cake slices, nori, and a soft-boiled egg (if using). Garnish with spring onions and sesame seeds and serve immediately.

The Message Unlike American and European-style short ribs, flanken-style or Korean-style ribs are cut lengthwise across the rib bones. They can be easily found, prepackaged, at Asian grocery stores.

Traditional Japanese ramen will use *tonkotsu* stock, a bone broth made with pork marrow or pork bone, simmered for 8–12 hours to coax out the most flavour. Nowadays, quality store-bought pork bone broth, or concentrated versions of it, can be found at larger supermarkets.

Marinated short ribs
3 cloves garlic, chopped
2 spring onions, chopped
4 slices ginger
½ Asian pear, unpeeled, cored, and cut into 1½-inch cubes
½ cup brown sugar
½ cup soy sauce or tamari
⅓ cup mirin
2 tsp sesame oil
1 lb *Certified Angus Beef* flanken-style short ribs (see note)

Ramen with L.A. kalbi
Marinated Short Ribs (see here)
1 lb ramen, udon, or thin wonton noodles
6 cups hot pork bone stock (see note)
4–6 slices Japanese spiral fish cakes (narutomaki)
2 sheets nori, cut in thirds
2 soft-boiled eggs, halved (optional)
1 spring onion, chopped
Toasted white sesame seeds, for garnish

GETTING JIGGY WITH IT: HUSTLE, FLOW, AND NEW CREATIONS

By 2016, with the fanfare surrounding my restaurants Kanpai and Yatai, the fried chicken, and the ramen burger, the world was my oyster. I travelled abroad at every opportunity, collaborated with chefs and food producers, and opened my eyes to new cooking methods and interpretations of food.

From Calgary to Barcelona to Palermo, I explored flavours new to me and began to lay a groundwork of the ideas introduced to me as a cook and entrepreneur. In developing recipes, I wanted to celebrate their roots. The recipes that follow reflect the amazing lessons and stories I've picked up along the way, and acknowledge cultural approaches to food.

Being raised in a diversity-rich country like Canada afforded me access to many types of cultures and food. Preserving the authenticity of original flavours is a celebration of both communities and heritage. When I make a ceviche (page 39), I want to create a recipe that's as close to how it'd be prepared in Peru (with plenty of cilantro, lime, and chiles). If I'm making beef and barley (page 122), it is as much a salute to those iconic Canadian ingredients as it is to the farmers who brought them to my kitchen.

By the same token, I hope that if someone were going to make a Chinese dish, they would consider how the ingredients are used traditionally and where they are sourced. I'm proud of my heritage, and I am honoured when I can cook something from other cultures, too.

My friend Chef Tawfik Shehata is an Egyptian Canadian who spent much of his childhood hanging out in Toronto's Chinatown. We often chat about Chinese ingredients, and I'm grateful I can learn from him. To me, the exchange is a perfect example of how individuals with different stories and backgrounds can discuss common interests at the table and pay tribute to one another.

Chinese Sausage Croquetas (page 30)

Ginger–Green Tea Beef with Cilantro-Ginger Aioli and Crispy Noodles (page 134)

Nashville Hot Chicken Sandwich (page 90)

The New Canadian Beef and Barley (page 122)

Red Quinoa and Sweet Potato Hash (page 64)

Taipei Ceviche with Taro Crisps (page 39)

Tandoori Masala Chicken Fried Rice (page 151)

Three-Nations Chicken (page 92)

良朋共煮

COOKING WITH FRIENDS

CROATIAN PANCAKES (*PALACINKE*)

RECIPE FROM
Marian Staresinic

A classically trained chef and partner of a successful food PR agency, Marian Staresinic has been a tremendous advocate and connector in the industry and has had a big impact on my career. She has paved roads for me, whether it was my exploring the Prairies with amazing agricultural producers or attending Spanish culinary events hosted by Michelin-star chef Ferran Adrià. Marian and I also share the values of memory-making and community-building within the food industry.

Palacinke (pah-lah-CHEEN-keh) is a traditional Croatian crepe that can be served plain or filled with cheese or a favourite jam. "When I was growing up, my mom would create it whenever we had guests over," Marian reveals. "Years later, she continues to make it for us whenever we visit. It's my honour to share a piece of my childhood here in this book."

Batter In a bowl, whisk together all ingredients, using a hand-held mixer. Let stand for 1–2 hours.

Cheese filling Combine all ingredients in a medium bowl.

Assembly Preheat oven to 350°F.

Heat 1 teaspoon oil in a 6-inch frying pan over medium-high heat. Pour 3 tablespoons batter into the pan. Tilt the pan to spread the batter (or, using the back of a spoon, swirl the batter in a circular motion to spread it) over the entire surface. Cook for 2–3 minutes, until crepe is browned. Flip over and cook for another 2–3 minutes. Keep warm in the oven and repeat with remaining batter.

Placing a few spoonfuls of filling on the lighter coloured side of the crepes, roll each up, and place seam side down in a baking dish. Bake for 10 minutes, then serve immediately.

Makes 10–14 crepes (varies based on desired thickness)

VEG
Prep 15 min, plus 1–2 hr standing time
Cook 30 minutes

Batter
1 cup all-purpose flour
¼ cup sugar
3 eggs
1½ cups whole milk
2 Tbsp melted butter
1 tsp grated lemon zest
⅛ tsp salt

Cheese filling
1 lb 2% cottage cheese
1 lb ricotta cheese
½ lb cream cheese
Sugar to taste (optional)

Assembly
Canola oil, for frying
Batter (see here)
Cheese Filling (see here) or your favourite jam

The Message Marian's mother often filled half the crepes with cheese and the other half with jam. That just gives us the perfect excuse to eat more than one.

FARM-STYLE TUSCAN SOUP

RECIPE FROM
Will Bergmann

Will Bergmann, also known as Will the Farmer or WTF, is a second-generation farmer based outside Winnipeg. A man of many hats (urban agriculturist, dad, husband, coffee roaster, restaurant owner, and real-time food producer), he taught me about agriculture, how to ice-fish, and to respect the food that eventually ends up on our plates.

I visit Will once a year to learn more about the land he tends to and the harvests he provides to his community. We spend those days fishing on the frozen ice of Lake Winnipeg and share amazing food stories. Because of Will, I have immense appreciation for our nation's producers and what it takes to get wholesome ingredients onto our tables.

This recipe from Will's mom adapts a classic Italian soup to Canadian flavours. "This hearty soup is a harvest-end celebration, full of garden produce and homemade sausage," Will shares. "It warms me up as much as it did when I was a kid returning to the house after a day in the field with my dad. It has always signalled a change in seasons and a time to slow down."

In a frying pan, add bacon and cook for 5–6 minutes, until crisp. Transfer to a bowl, along with the grease.

In a heavy-bottomed saucepan set over medium-high heat, add sausage and cook for 10–12 minutes, until browned. Add onions and garlic and sauté for 1–2 minutes, until slightly browned. Add potatoes, stock, and 4 cups water and bring mixture to a boil. Reduce heat to medium and simmer for 10–12 minutes, until potatoes are softened. Stir in bacon and grease and simmer for 10 minutes.

Add kale and cream and cook for another 4–5 minutes. Ladle into bowls and garnish with chili flakes.

Serves 4

GF
Prep 10 min
Cook 45 min

½ (375-g) package bacon, sliced
1 ring smoky farmer sausage, chopped into bite-sized pieces
1 onion, finely chopped
2 cloves garlic, finely chopped
2 large potatoes
2 cups chicken stock
2 cups kale, stems removed and chopped
1 cup heavy cream
Chili flakes, for garnish

WILD MUSHROOM ARANCINI

RECIPE FROM
Keith Hoare

Chef Keith Hoare is a caterer turned culinarian, a high school instructor, mentor, and life influencer. The 2014 recipient of the Toronto Star Teacher of the Year award, he dedicates his life to guiding high school students in a technical culinary program at Thistletown Collegiate Institute (TCI), in the Toronto suburb of Rexdale (incidentally, my hometown).

He is relentless in his quest to provide students with access to memorable culinary travels through a program funded in part by his philanthropic work in local shelters and with at-risk communities. A past *Chopped* contestant and winner, Chef Keith donated all his winnings to fund his students' culinary trips. And his Chef Harvest Garden Party is one event where the city's top chefs line up to say yes and participate in a worthy and charitable cause.

This dish, created by his students, is the product of his efforts and legacy with the school and the community. The recipe was kitchen tested by the culinary students of TCI.

Rice balls Heat oil in a large saucepan over medium-high heat. Add onions, garlic, mushrooms, and thyme and cook for 7 minutes, until onions are translucent. Stir in rice and season with salt and pepper. Pour in 2 cups stock and stir continuously, until the rice has absorbed most of the liquid. Ladle in another 1 cup or so, repeating process until all the stock is used and rice is fully cooked, plump, and creamy (about 20 minutes). Transfer rice to a baking sheet and fold in Parmesan and butter. Let cool.

Using a ¼-cup scoop, form a rice ball, then press your finger into its centre and insert a heaping teaspoon of mozzarella. Pinch the rice to enclose. Repeat with remaining rice and mozzarella. (Alternatively, you can use your hands. Dip your hands in a bowl of cold water, then roll the rice into balls about 1½ inches in diameter.)

Makes 20 arancini

VEG
Prep 35 min,
plus 1 hr chilling time
Cook 45 min

Rice balls
2 Tbsp olive oil
¼ onion, finely chopped
3 cloves garlic, finely chopped
¼ cup chopped cremini mushrooms
¼ cup dried wild mushrooms, soaked and chopped
½ Tbsp dried thyme
1 cup Arborio rice
½ Tbsp salt
½ Tbsp black pepper
3½ cups hot vegetable stock
1 cup grated Parmesan
2 Tbsp cold butter, cut into ½-inch cubes
¾ cup shredded mozzarella

Breading In a bowl, combine ½ cup flour, ½ tablespoon garlic powder, ½ tablespoon parsley, ¾ teaspoon salt, and ¾ teaspoon pepper. Place eggs in another bowl. In the third bowl, combine panko breadcrumbs and the remaining flour, ½ tablespoon garlic powder, ½ tablespoon parsley, ¾ teaspoon salt, and ¾ teaspoon pepper.

Dip a rice ball in the flour mixture, then in the egg and the breadcrumb mixture to coat. Repeat with the remaining arancini. Chill for 1 hour to firm up.

Assembly Heat oil in a deep fryer or deep saucepan over medium-high heat to 375°F. Using a metal slotted spoon, carefully lower arancini into the oil, working in batches to avoid overcrowding, and deep-fry for 4–6 minutes, until golden brown. Transfer arancini to a plate lined with paper towel to drain. Sprinkle with Parmesan and serve.

Breading
1 cup all-purpose flour (divided)
1 Tbsp garlic powder (divided)
1 Tbsp dried parsley (divided)
½ Tbsp salt (divided)
½ Tbsp black pepper (divided)
3 eggs, beaten
1 cup panko breadcrumbs

Assembly
Canola oil, for deep-frying
Parmesan, for sprinkling

BAKED MAC AND CHEESE

RECIPE FROM
Jasmine Baker

Jasmine Baker, a good friend and a peer, is an advocate for food producers and chefs, and for equality in professional kitchens. I've had the privilege to partner with her to produce food-based educational programs for some of Canada's most renowned chefs at the Royal Agricultural Winter Fair in Toronto. Budding foodies and marquee chefs came together for ten days of culinary learning.

Jasmine is truly a driving force for all that is good in the food industry, and it brings me great pleasure to showcase her cozy, delicious, and soul-feeding recipe for a classic mac 'n' cheese.

Preheat oven to 375°F.

Bring a large saucepan of heavily salted water to a boil. Add pasta and cook for 2–3 minutes less than the package directs. (Pasta should be undercooked, since it will continue to cook in the cheese sauce.) Scoop out 1 cup pasta water and reserve. Drain pasta and rinse under cold running water.

Melt 4 tablespoons butter in a large heavy-bottomed saucepan over medium-low heat. Whisk in flour and cook for 2–3 minutes, until golden and fragrant. Stir in mustard powder.

Whisk in milk, then bring mixture to a boil. Add bay leaf, reduce heat to medium-low, and simmer for 4–5 minutes, whisking occasionally until sauce is thick enough to coat the back of a wooden spoon. Remove bay leaf. Stir in salt, nutmeg, cayenne, and pepper.

Add Gruyère, cheddar, and ½ cup Parmesan and whisk until combined and melted. (If the sauce is too thick and difficult to mix, slowly add enough reserved pasta water to loosen.) Add pasta and mix to coat.

Transfer mixture to a large baking dish. Sprinkle evenly with the remaining ½ cup Parmesan and panko breadcrumbs. Melt the remaining 2 tablespoons butter and pour over the panko. Bake for 20–30 minutes, until the topping is golden.

Serves 6–8

VEG
Prep 10 min
Cook 40–50 min

1 lb short pasta, such as elbow pasta, penne, or shells
6 Tbsp (¾ stick) butter (divided)
½ cup all-purpose flour
1 tsp mustard powder
4 cups 2% milk
1 bay leaf
1 tsp salt
¼ tsp freshly grated or ground nutmeg
Pinch of cayenne pepper
Pinch of black pepper
2 cups grated Gruyère
1 cup shredded aged cheddar
1 cup grated Parmesan (divided)
1 cup panko breadcrumbs

The Message Most cheese shops will grate cheese for you if you can spare the time. Avoid packaged shredded cheeses, which lack flavour.

OLIVES, VERDIAL VARIETY

RECIPE FROM
The Adrià brothers

The Adrià brothers taught me that many cultures (including those of China and Korea) eat tapas-style dishes. When I had the opportunity to cook for Albert Adrià in Toronto, he asked me many questions about the flavours and techniques of our dishes. I realized then that although we have cultural differences, we share a zest and passion for the same things.

This recipe is for the iconic spherical olive made popular at El Bulli, the Adrià brothers' restaurant in Spain. I am so humbled and grateful to Chef Ferran, Chef Albert, and the Estrella Damm team for allowing us to feature this recipe in the book.

Olive juice Purée the olives with a hand-held mixer. Strain purée through a fine-mesh sieve. Place in a vacuum bag, seal, and refrigerate until needed. (The olive juice can also be used as a sauce for many other dishes, such as salads, jellies, and cocktails.)

Spherical olive base Combine olive juice and calcium salt in a blender and blend until salt is dissolved. Add xanthan gum and blend again until smooth. Refrigerate for 24 hours to eliminate the air bubbles. (Alternatively, speed up the process using a vacuum sealer.) Strain mixture. Transfer to a container and refrigerate.

Flavoured olive oil Open the head of garlic to extract the whole cloves with the skin intact. Put them unpeeled in a saucepan with 100 grams olive oil and slow simmer at 160°F for 1 hour. Remove from heat and let cool to room temperature. Add the remaining 300 grams oil, thyme, rosemary, lemon and orange zest, and peppercorns.

Serves 4

DF, GF, VEG
Prep 12 minutes, plus 24 hr chilling time
Cook 1 hour

Olive juice
450 g Verdial olives, drained and pitted

Spherical olive base
200 g Olive Juice (see here)
1.2 g calcium salt (Calcic)
0.7 g xanthan gum

Flavoured olive oil
20 g garlic
400 g extra-virgin olive oil (divided)
¼ sprig thyme
¼ sprig rosemary
Grated zest of 1 lemon
Grated zest of 1 orange
2.5 g black peppercorns

Alginate bath Mix water and alginate in a blender until alginate is fully dissolved, then strain into a bowl. Refrigerate for 24 hours to eliminate the air bubbles. (Alternatively, speed up the process using a vacuum sealer.)

Assembly Fill a container with alginate bath, about 2 inches deep. Using a 5-ml spherical spoon, carefully drop the spherical olive base into the alginate bath to form each spherical olive. Don't let the olives touch each other. Leave olives in the alginate bath for 1 minute. Using a slotted spoon, remove olives and carefully rinse in water. In a bowl, combine olives and flavoured olive oil. Refrigerate until serving.

Divide olives and flavoured oil into 4 small jars. Serve the olives together with a slotted spoon at the table.

Alginate bath
500 g mineral water
2.5 g alginate (algin)

Assembly
Alginate Bath (see here)
Spherical Olive Base (see here)
Flavoured Olive Oil (see here)
Mineral water

"HENRY GOES TO KANPAI" TAIWANESE CHEESEBOARD

RECIPE FROM
Afrim Pristine

This collaboration between me and cheese master Afrim Pristine is one of the first Asian-inspired cheeses to hit the market. A mild goat cheese is rolled in a medley of sencha green tea, mandarin lime zest, toasted black rice, and junmai sake, then aged to perfection. Asian-inspired jam, poached fruit, and Chinese bread complete the cheeseboard.

Berry compote Combine ½ cup sugar and ½ cup water in a saucepan over medium heat. Stir until the sugar is dissolved. Add berries and lemon juice and reduce heat to low. Cook for 15–20 minutes, stirring occasionally. If desired, add a pinch of salt for extra seasoning. Remove from heat and let cool.

Bring wine and the remaining ⅓ cup sugar to a boil in a separate saucepan over medium heat. Add Thai basil, star anise, lemongrass, and ½ cup water. Add pears, reduce heat to medium-low, and cook uncovered for 30 minutes. Remove pears and let cool. Let compote cool.

Bao Heat oil in a deep saucepan over high heat. Carefully lower mantou into the oil and deep-fry for 4–5 minutes, until they float to the surface and are golden brown. Transfer to a plate lined with paper towel to drain and cool. Slice each into 3–4 pieces.

Assembly Place cheese rondelle on a serving platter. Arrange poached pears, bao, and bowls of the berry compote and honey on the board and serve.

The Message Mantou is a soft, white steamed bread popular in Northern China. It is commonly steamed or deep-fried and served with condensed milk as a dipping sauce. You can find it in the refrigerator or freezer sections of Asian supermarkets. Alternatively, substitute it with open-faced bao or slices of fresh baguette.

In Toronto, this cheese can sometimes be found as a special feature at The Cheese Boutique, but a modified, simpler version can be made at home by soaking mild soft goat cheese in sake with 1½ tablespoons green tea powder for 48 hours. Pat dry before serving.

Serves 4

VEG
Prep 15 min
Cook 50 min

Berry compote
½ cup + ⅓ cup sugar (divided)
2 cups seasonal berries
1¼ tsp lemon juice
Pinch of salt (optional)
½ cup wine
6 Thai basil sprigs
1 star anise
½ stalk lemongrass, trimmed and peeled
1 pear (preferably Asian), halved and cored

Bao
4 mantou (see note)
4 cups canola oil, for deep-frying

Assembly
1 (9-oz) rondelle Henry Goes to Kanpai (see note)
¼ cup local honey

FAVA FALAFELS

RECIPE FROM
Tawfik Shehata

Chef Tawfik Shehata and I first met on a culinary trip to learn about poultry farming. Years later, I hired him as executive chef, and a friendship was immediately formed.

As a former farmer, an agricultural ambassador, and a part-time culinary instructor, Egyptian Canadian Chef Tawfik wears many proverbial toques and is one of the most knowledgeable chefs I know. In his childhood, he spent many a day in Toronto's Chinatown, where his mother taught English to Chinese children. As a result, our memories of Chinese food in Toronto are similar. For me, these shared, multicultural experiences make up the perfect immigrant story.

This Shehata family heirloom, passed down from generation to generation, is offered here in loving memory of his mother. I'm honoured to feature it in the book.

Drain fava beans, then rinse under cold running water. In a food processor, pulse beans to a coarse meal. Transfer to a large bowl.

Toast coriander seeds in a frying pan over medium-low heat for 1–2 minutes, stirring occasionally, until slightly darkened. Add cumin seeds and toast for 30 seconds, until darkened. Set aside to cool.

Using a clean coffee grinder (or a pestle and mortar), grind seeds to a powder. Add to beans, stirring to mix.

Makes 28 falafels

DF, GF, VEG
Prep 15 minutes, plus 24 hr soaking time
Cook 10–15 minutes

2 cups dried fava beans, shelled, soaked in water for 24 hours
3 Tbsp coriander seeds
2 Tbsp cumin seeds
1 onion, quartered
6 cloves garlic, finely chopped
1¼ cups chopped cilantro, leaves and tender stems
1 cup chopped Italian parsley
1 Tbsp salt
Pinch of cayenne pepper (optional)
1 tsp sesame seeds
Vegetable oil, for frying
Hummus, garlic sauce, pita, rice, or tabbouleh, to serve

In a food processor, combine onions, garlic, cilantro, and parsley. Add mixture to beans, then stir in salt and cayenne (if using). (At this point, you can freeze the mixture in an airtight container for up to 1 month. When ready to use, simply defrost in the fridge.)

Shape 2 tablespoons mixture into a ball. Using your thumb, gently press a few sesame seeds into centre of each, then flatten to form patties, about 2 inches in diameter.

Heat oil in heavy saucepan, about ½ inch deep, to a temperature of 350°F. Add falafels, working in batches to avoid overcrowding, and cook for 1–1½ minutes on each side until darkened. (Turn once only.) Transfer to a plate lined with paper towel to drain.

Serve warm or at room temperature, with hummus, garlic sauce, pita, rice, or tabbouleh.

MRS. ARNETTE'S SPINACH PIE

RECIPE FROM
Mrs. Arnette

I met one of my best friends, Daryl, in the mid-nineties, and we were thick as thieves—first as colleagues, then as roommates and eventually in a brotherhood. On my first visit to his family home in East Jersey, his mother, a talented home cook, had prepared a slew of heirloom recipes in anticipation of our arrival. There was whole roasted turkey, mac 'n' cheese, and cornbread, but the most memorable was her Southern-style spinach pie. From that day forward, I always asked Daryl, whenever he went to visit, to bring back some pie. I am so honoured to share this recipe with the world. Thank you, Mrs. Arnette.

Filling Heat 1 tablespoon butter in a medium saucepan over medium-high heat. Add spinach and sauté for 3–4 minutes, until wilted and softened. Drain spinach well, then transfer to a large bowl. (It should amount to about 3 cups.) Add the remaining 3 tablespoons butter and fold. Set aside.

In a mixing bowl, combine eggs and both cheeses.

Heat oil in a large frying pan over medium-high heat. Add onions and sauté for 5 minutes, until softened and translucent. Set aside to cool. Once cooled, add to egg mixture, fold in spinach, and season with salt, pepper, and oregano. Mix thoroughly.

Serves 4

VEG
Prep 15 min,
plus 1 hr chilling time
Cook 55 min

Filling
4 Tbsp (½ stick) butter,
    softened (divided)
3 lbs spinach
4 eggs, beaten
2 cups shredded cheddar
2 cups shredded mozzarella
2 Tbsp canola oil
1 onion, chopped
½ tsp salt
½ tsp black pepper
¼ tsp dried oregano

Pie crust In a large bowl, sift together flour and salt. Using a pastry blender or fork, cut shortening into flour mixture until shortening pieces are pea-sized. Gradually add 1 cup ice-cold water, 1 tablespoon at a time, stirring with the fork just until dough holds together and forms a smooth ball. Cover with plastic wrap and chill for 1 hour.

Preheat oven to 375°F. Brush an 8-inch baking dish with butter or oil.

Divide dough into two equal portions. On a lightly floured work surface, roll out dough large enough to cover the bottom and sides of the pan with a ½-inch overhang. Carefully place in the pan and scoop in filling.

Roll out the second portion of dough to fit on top of the pie. Roll the overhang from the bottom pastry over the top and seal.

Lightly brush top pastry with butter, then bake for 50–55 minutes, until top of the pie is golden brown and the edges are crisped. Allow pie to set at room temperature for 15 minutes before serving.

Pie crust
3¼ cups all-purpose flour, plus extra for dusting
1 tsp salt
1 cup vegetable shortening
Melted butter, for greasing and brushing

MRS. ARNETTE'S SPINACH PIE (PAGE 184)

SOLE TO SOUL

Now, one might argue that sneakers have no place in a cookbook. But whoever says that doesn't know me, nor my obsession with kicks, nor my formative years of yearning for, but never being able to have, cool sneakers.

It isn't just me. Look around the kitchen and you'll be amazed at how many cooks play basketball and love sneakers. Hip hop is in our blood (and for most of my ventures, it's been on the soundtrack, too). My online video series *Soulful Food Stories* has given me a platform to utilize food as a gateway to culture, and it's important to me to start every episode on my feet. The show has also given me a platform from which to express my appreciation for something that I could only admire from a distance as a young child of immigrant parents with limited resources—cool kicks.

Call them a tribute to young Trevor, or my ode to my basketball-obsessed grandfather, who never lived to see the Toronto Raptors win an NBA Championship (I could have written an entire book about *that* 2019 moment). Growing up, they were beyond my reach. Now, as a grown-ass man, I can afford to buy them.

When I began to make public appearances, whether on television or online, I made sure that an epic pair of kicks was always a part of my outfit. I'd often be found wearing them while cooking on the line, and I can be seen on *Cityline*, with Tracy Moore, wearing bright Jordans. For me, my foot candy is like a chef's personalized apron or chef coat.

雞尾酒

COCK-
TAILS

BEST I EVER HAD

My wife's favourite musical artist is Drizzy "6-God" Drake, hence the name of this cocktail. This drink melds spirits from Mexico, the Caribbean and—even farther south—Brazil, making it a refreshing complement to tacos or ceviche.

Put 1 handful of ice in a shaker, then add all ingredients except bitters. Shake for 1 minute. Strain into a rock glass over the remaining ice. Top with bitters and garnish with lime twist.

Serves 1

DF, GF, QUICK, VEG
Prep 5 min

2 handfuls of ice cubes (divided)
2 oz grapefruit juice
1 oz Ancho Reyes
½ oz spiced rum
½ oz Pitú Cachaça
1 oz lime juice
3–4 dashes of bitters
Lime twist, for garnish

BARCA RADLER

This perfect summer beverage combines the light hoppiness of Spanish beer and the fresh citrus notes of grapefruit. I'd say it's almost *too* easy to drink.

Put ice in a pint glass. Pour beer slowly and gently over the ice, minimizing the foam. Pour in grapefruit juice, then add bitters. Garnish with grapefruit slice.

Serves 1

DF, QUICK, VEG
Prep 5 min

Handful of ice cubes
1 (12-oz) bottle lager beer
   (I prefer an Estrella Damm)
½ cup strained grapefruit juice
2 drops bitters
Grapefruit slice, for garnish

THE BEST I EVER HAD (PAGE 190)

BIG DADDY SUGAR CANE

This is a shout-out to the "smooth operator" himself, one of the greatest emcees of all time, Big Daddy Kane. A unique blend of sweet and sour notes makes this an aperitif for any time of the year.

Muddle mint leaves and lemon juice in a shaker. Add rum, Chartreuse, sugar cane juice, and ice. Shake vigorously, then strain into a coupe glass. Garnish with lemon twist and sour cherry.

Serves 1

DF, GF, QUICK, VEG
Prep 5 min

Mint leaves
1 oz lemon juice
1½ oz amber rum
½ oz yellow Chartreuse
2 oz sugar cane juice
Handful of ice cubes
Angostura bitters
Lemon twist, for garnish
Sour cherry, for garnish

TURN THE LIGHTS DOWN LOW

I was listening to the Lauren Hill and Bob Marley track of the same name when I created this alcohol-free drink. This refreshing tropical blend ends with the sweet burn of ginger beer at the tail end of a sip.

Muddle mint and ginger in a shaker. Add pineapple juice, lime juice, and 1 handful of ice and shake vigorously. Strain into a highball glass over the remaining ice. Add the muddled mint and ginger. Top with ginger beer and garnish with lemon twist.

Serves 1

DF, GF, QUICK, VEG
Prep 5 min

Handful of mint leaves
Slice of ginger
3 oz pineapple juice
1 oz lime juice
2 handfuls of ice cubes (divided)
3 oz ginger beer
Lemon twist, for garnish

INSIDE OUT

While creating new cocktail lists, I wanted a cocktail informed by ingredients with redeeming qualities. The detoxifying probiotic elements of kombucha and the smokiness of mezcal combine with fresh fruit garnishes to create this twenty-first-century elixir.

Agave syrup In a small saucepan, combine agave nectar and 1 cup water and bring to a boil. Reduce heat to medium-low and simmer for 20 minutes, until mixture is reduced by a third. Remove from heat, then chill. (Any leftover syrup can be stored in an airtight container in the refrigerator for up to 10 days.)

Muddle mint and grapefruit juice in a shaker. Add mezcal, agave syrup, and 1 handful of ice and shake vigorously. Strain into a highball glass over the remaining ice. Add muddled mint. Top with kombucha and garnish with mint.

Serves 1

DF, GF, VEG
Prep 10 min
Cook 20 min

Agave syrup
⅓ cup agave nectar

Mint leaves, plus extra
  for garnish
2 oz grapefruit juice
2 oz smoky mezcal
1½ oz Agave Syrup (see here)
2 handfuls of ice cubes (divided)
2 oz ginger kombucha

THE HALLE BERRIES MOCKTAIL

A fresh take on a mocktail that makes you forget about the hard stuff. Perfect for that summer gathering or backyard fête, it's an excellent accompaniment to salads, light meals, and "Fun"day brunches. And yes, Halle Berry was my nineties celebrity crush!

Longan syrup In a small saucepan, combine longan, honey, and 1 cup water and bring to a boil. Reduce heat to medium-low and simmer for 40 minutes, until mixture is reduced by a third. Remove from heat, then chill. Strain. (Any leftover syrup can be stored in an airtight container in the refrigerator for up to 10 days.)

Muddle berries, syrup, and lemon juice in a shaker. Add 1 handful of ice and shake vigorously. Strain into a highball glass over the remaining ice. Top with soda water and garnish with mint.

Serves 1

DF, GF, VEG
Prep 10 min
Cook 40 min

Longan syrup
5 longan, peeled
⅓ cup local honey

4–5 blueberries, or
   berries of choice
2 oz Longan Syrup (see here)
2 oz lemon juice
2 handfuls of ice cubes (divided)
4 oz soda water
Sprig of fresh mint, for garnish

BONITA APPLEBUM

Named after a classic song by A Tribe Called Quest, this drink was created for my wife as a riff on the classic Pisco Sour.

(Use a fresh, preferably farm-fresh, egg in this recipe. Pregnant, elderly, or people with compromised immune systems should avoid consuming raw egg.)

Thai basil syrup In a pot, combine Thai basil, sugar, and 1 cup water and bring to a boil. Lower heat and simmer for at least 1 hour. Remove from heat, then chill. Strain.

Rim a coupe glass with lime juice and then sugar. Put the remaining ingredients except bitters in a shaker and shake vigorously. Strain into the coupe glass and spoon any egg foam remaining in the shaker on top. Top with bitters, swizzling into a design of your choice.

Serves 1

DF, GF, VEG
Prep 10 min
Cook 1 hr

Thai basil syrup
3 sprigs Thai basil, leaves and stems chopped
½ cup sugar

Lime juice, for rimming
Sugar, for rimming
Handful of ice cubes
1 oz pisco
1½ oz St-Germain elderflower liqueur
1½ oz gin
2 oz Thai Basil Syrup (see here)
1 oz lime juice
1 egg white
2 drops bitters

CRAZY RICH ASIANS

A new, Asian spin on a champagne-sparkling cocktail, this drink, which I love to serve at events and home cocktail parties, exudes confidence and commands attention with its vibrant colours and ingredients.

Green tea syrup In a small saucepan, combine sugar and 1 cup water. Add tea bag and bring mixture to a boil. Reduce heat to medium-low and simmer uncovered for 1 hour, until reduced by a third. Remove from heat, then chill. (Any leftover syrup can be stored in an airtight container in the refrigerator for up to 10 days.)

Put pisco, syrup, lemon juice, and ice in a shaker and shake vigorously. Place pomegranate seeds in a champagne flute, strain in pisco mixture, and top with sparkling wine.

Serves 1

DF, GF, VEG
Prep 10 min
Cook 1 hr

Green tea syrup
¼ cup sugar
1 green tea bag

2 oz pisco
2 oz Green Tea Syrup (see here)
1 oz lemon juice
Handful of ice cubes
5 pomegranate seeds
3 oz sparkling wine (preferably Crémant d'Alsace)

THE CHEATING COMMUNIST

I had help from old friend and successful bar owner Dustin Keating in creating this popular drink for Kanpai Snack Bar. Marrying Asian ingredients like Calpico soda and shochu, this drink is just plain old delicious.

Lemongrass syrup In a small saucepan, mix together lemongrass, sugar, and ½ cup water and bring to a boil. Reduce heat to medium-low and simmer for 1 hour, until mixture is reduced by a quarter. Remove from heat, then chill. Strain. (Any leftover syrup can be stored in an airtight container in the refrigerator for up to 10 days.)

Put 1 handful of ice and the remaining ingredients in a shaker and shake vigorously. Strain into a rock glass over the remaining ice. Garnish with chile.

Serves 1

DF, GF, VEG
Prep 10 min
Cook 1 hr

Lemongrass syrup
1 stalk lemongrass, trimmed and peeled, then chopped in thirds (½ cup)
½ cup sugar

2 handfuls of ice cubes (divided)
3 oz Calpico soda
1½ oz Tanaka Moonlight Shochu
½ oz Lillet
½ oz lime juice
½ oz Lemongrass Syrup (see here)
Bird's eye chile, skewered on bamboo, for garnish

THE BROHAM

This instant classic was inspired by a favourite drink at a friend's bar (yes, he gave me his blessing to provide the recipe here). At Kanpai we took it one step further by casking this cocktail so that we could be one of the first in the city to serve cocktails on tap.

Chai syrup In a small saucepan, combine honey and 1½ cups water. Add tea bag and bring mixture to a boil. Reduce heat to medium-low and simmer for 1 hour, until mixture is reduced by a third. Remove from heat, then chill. (Any leftover syrup can be stored in an airtight container in the refrigerator for up to 10 days.)

Gently muddle cucumber in a shaker. Add mezcal, syrup, lime juice, and 1 handful of ice in a shaker and shake vigorously. Strain into a rock glass over the remaining ice and top with ginger beer.
Garnish with cucumber slice and lime wedge.

Serves 1

DF, GF, VEG
Prep 10 min
Cook 1 hr

Chai syrup
2 Tbsp local honey
1 chai tea bag

4 slices peeled seedless
    cucumber (each ¼-inch-thick)
2 oz mezcal
1 oz Chai Syrup (see here)
1 oz lime juice
2 handfuls of ice cubes (divided)
2½ oz ginger beer
Skewered cucumber slice,
    for garnish
Lime wedge, for garnish

OOH LONG ISLAND ICED TEA

Here's my take on the classic Long Island Iced Tea, traditionally a lottery of spirits. This easy-drinking elixir features an array of Chinese aromatics, leaving the old, dated version behind.

Lemongrass ooh long tea In a saucepan, stir together lemongrass, sugar, and 1 cup water. Add tea bags and bring mixture to a boil. Reduce heat to medium-low and simmer for 1 hour. Remove from heat, then chill. Strain.

Put iced tea, gin, rum, lychee liquor, tequila, and 1 handful of ice in a shaker and shake vigorously. Strain into a highball glass over the remaining ice. Top with tonic and garnish with lemon wheel.

Serves 1

DF, GF, VEG
Prep 10 min
Cook 1 hr

Lemongrass ooh long iced tea
1 stalk lemongrass, trimmed, peeled, and chopped
2 Tbsp sugar or local honey
2 oolong tea bags

2 oz Lemongrass Ooh Long Iced Tea (see here)
½ oz gin
½ oz rum
½ oz lychee liquor
½ oz tequila
2 handfuls of ice cubes (divided)
2 oz Fever Tree Sicilian Lemon tonic
Dehydrated lemon wheel, for garnish

HIP-HOP INK: THE LOVE OF INK, BEATS, AND LIBATIONS

As you might have gleaned from reading this book, I'm in a "give no fucks" phase of my life, which is exhilarating. It means I'm getting tattoos of eggs and tacos and sneakers on the regular, but it also means that I'm going to dedicate an entire chapter to amazing cocktails, ink, and hip hop (quite the trifecta, if you ask me). Call it a chapter about vibes, but my first book wouldn't be complete without a shout-out to a few of my favourite things.

Hip hop has been the soundtrack to my life, and in a way, it's been the soundtrack to the city of Toronto, too. If you grew up in a certain era, you listened to the same music as everyone else here—people from all walks of life and neighbourhoods. The food and drink at my restaurants have always been synonymous with epic tunes, from Public Enemy to Jay-Z, and I loved watching guys in suits snacking on fried chicken while rapping along to NWA's *Straight Outta Compton*.

Recently, I got a tattoo of the Larry O'Brien NBA Championship Trophy, with a Biggie crown affixed on top—after all, nobody wears a crown better than he did. I waited my whole damn life for that moment, and it means a lot to me. Grandpa TK loved basketball. We would watch the "Showtime" Lakers on Sundays. The 2019 championship for my hometown Raptors brought back many fond memories.

It felt like a fitting big up to the city that raised me, and I hope this book feels the same way for you. There are stories for all the tattoos I have, most having something to do with food, and important enough to take with me forever. The drinks featured in this chapter came out of some of the most popular creations people shared with me during our dining experiences together. Here I've curated the beverages with carefully considered ingredients, names, and accompanying soundtrack. This is, in part, how I want to create new stories and memories around food. And here I share them with you.

ACKNOWLEDGEMENTS

To my amazing family, and in particular Mom and Dad, who accepted the good and bad and ensured the best bites got onto my plate rather than their own. To my sister, Stephanie, who was a force on this project in many more ways than one; this story is just as much about you. To my beautiful daughter, Cassaundra, I cherish our fun meals together and finding the best churros and bubble tea spots to share. I will always remember Lil' C's café in the basement, featuring your favourite table d'hôte menu. To all the amazing partners who jumped in to be a part of this book, thank you. To Sean and Marian of Branding & Buzzing, thank you for the collaborations and partnerships through the years; it's been fun doing so much together. To Brione, what started off as a quick video interview spawned into an amazing set of stories we have shared with the world. To friends that inspired me and contributed to this book, I'm so honoured to share your stories among mine. To Chef Josef Vonlanthan, it was into your kitchen that I first set foot at that first hotel job; I never forgot the wise words you shared, RIP. To Annie, Tim, and Michael, three of the best in hospitality, your mentorship through the years helped me grow in so many ways; you said yes to me when many said no. To those that believed in me... and doubted me; you inspired and drove me in very different ways. To all of those who once or continue to work in this industry, it's as imperfect a world as can be but I couldn't think of doing anything else. Thank you to each and every person on a line, behind a bar, in the pit: you are the heart and soul of a beautiful symphony.

And to the one and only Aneeta, my wife and best friend; I will walk to the ends of the earth with you to find that perfect slice of pizza and scrumptious cheeseburger... with a nice glass of bubbly, of course. I love you more than any meal.

INDEX

About the author

Trevor's life and career have been surrounded by the sights and sounds of food. For the past twenty years, he has produced thousands of event experiences and has helped co-create and develop some of Toronto's foremost food brands, including Kanpai Snack Bar, Yatai Japanese Street Food, Shook Noodle, La Brea Food, Makan Noodle Bar, Joybird Fried Chicken & Side Things, and his catering and hospitality brand, Pop Kitchen. His culinary agency, Highbell Group, organizes uniquely immersive culinary events that push the boundaries of innovation. Trevor is a frequent consultant, speaker, and editorial contributor to media outlets such as *Cityline* and to business forums. He also directs and hosts a video series called *Soulful Food Stories*. He lives in Toronto and is a proud husband and father to Aneeta and Cassaundra. This is his first book.